Behind the Razor Wire

Portrait of a Contemporary American Prison System

Behind the Razor Wire
Portrait of a Contemporary American Prison System

Photographs and text by Michael Jacobson-Hardy

Foreword by Angela Y. Davis

Essays by John Edgar Wideman, Marc Mauer, and
James Gilligan, M.D.

New York University Press
NEW YORK AND LONDON

NEW YORK UNIVERSITY PRESS

New York and London

© 1999 by New York University

© 1999 Photographs by Michael Jacobson-Hardy

© 1999 foreword by Angela Y. Davis

All rights reserved

Library of Congress Cataloging -in-Publications Data
    Jacobson-Hardy, Michael, 1951–
        Behind the razor wire: portrait of a contemporary American
    prison system / photographs and text by Michael Jacobson-
    Hardy; foreword by Angela Y. Davis; essays by John Edgar
    Wideman, Marc Mauer, and James Gilligan.
        p.   cm.
    ISBN 0-8147-2430-8 (alk. paper)
    1. Prisons—United States.   2. Prisons—United States—
    Pictorial works.   3. Criminal justice. Administration of—
    United States.   4. Criminal Justice. Administration of—
    United States—Pictorial works.   I. Title.
    HV9471.J32   1998
    365'.973—dc21   98-24771
                                                               CIP

New York University Press books are printed on acid-free paper,
and their binding materials are chosen for strength and durability.

Manufactured in the United States of America

10   9   8   7   6   5   4   3   2   1

Contents

Acknowledgments

I would like to thank the following individuals and organizations for helping to make this project possible. Thanks to Marc Mauer, John Edgar Wideman, Dr. James Gilligan, and Angela Davis for their insightful essays and to the people in prison who agreed to be photographed. I want to especially thank Robin Bavaro and the people at the Massachusetts Department of Correction for giving me clearance and providing me with security while I photographed inside several state prisons.

Peter Chalapatis was generous with his time at MCI–Gardner. Erin Keaney and Lieutenant Jim Satori accompanied me while I photographed at the Deer Island jail. Lieutenant Virginia Land was generous with her time at MCI–Framingham. Richard McCarthy and William Toller were kind enough to facilitate my work at Hampden County House of Correction, both at the old York Street jail in Springfield and at the new jail in Ludlow. Deputy Frank Godek made it possible for me to interview and photograph inmates at Hampshire County House of Correction. Paul Dickaut gave me an impromptu tour at MCI–Lancaster. I want to thank Martin Bander for providing assistance at the Charles Street Jail and to John Marshall for his tour of MCI–Cedar-Junction.

Thanks to the many people who guided me with their insights and encouragement, including Walter Silva, Dorothy Walsh, Luke Janusz, Jennie Traschen, David Kastor, and members of the Western Massachusetts Prison Issues Group. Thanks to Thomas Dumm, William Newman, Phyllis Kornfeld, David Hoose, Robert Weir, Betsy Siersma, Ellen Lawrence, the Harburg Foundation, the HKH Foundation, the Solidago Foundation, Available Potential

Enterprises, Linda and Alan Eccleston, George Levinger, Andrew Jacobson, Carol Bernstein Ferry, Hosie Baskin, Sara Buttonweiser, James Campbell, Tom Asher, Jim Levey, Jennifer Ladd, Robby Meeropol, Robert Winston, and Clark Dougan. I especially want to thank Eric Zinner, my editor at New York University Press, for his enthusiasm and encouragement. My deepest appreciation is to my wife, Ruth, whose love and support sustain my work.

Michael Jacobson-Hardy

Foreword

A World unto Itself: Multiple Invisibilities of Imprisonment

ANGELA Y. DAVIS

As I first perused the photographs included in this volume, I was struck—as I am repeatedly in my work as a prison activist—by the profound contrast between the self-possession that characterizes so many prisoners and the social dispossession to which they are subjected, individually and collectively, as wards of the penal system. The remarkable portraits Michael Jacobson-Hardy has made inside prisons in Massachusetts represent visual evidence of invisible populations, invisible worlds: prisoners, cells, bars, corridors, guards, gates, doors, work settings (where, among other things, American flags are produced), and external landscapes—exercise yards, gun towers—all surrounded by cyclone fences and layer upon layer of razor wire.

The razor wire functions, both metaphorically and materially, as a universal symbol of suspended liberty. It marks the end of the free world and the beginning of the imprisoned world, a world far removed from the outside, where those of us who are "free" have the luxury of being able to take our liberty for granted. The psychological impact of razor wire is as potent as its potential physical impact; its bizarre and uncommon appearance, its seemingly benign roundness belying its vicious jagged edge, is enough to transfix any onlooker, at least momentarily. What person who has stood outside a jail or prison has not marveled at the difficulty posed by that razor wire for the would-be escapee? This is, after all, its supreme purpose. Who has stood on the perimeter of a prison without imagining the effects of razor wire against flesh?

And then again, how many of us *have* stood outside such an institution, let alone inside one? This is a question that quickly separates people of color—particularly black people—from whites, and the poor from the affluent. Most people in this country do not have direct knowledge of the penal system, although the prison has inhabited the personal and political histories of black and poor people continually. Most people probably have not pondered the razor wire and certainly have not tried to evoke concretely in their imaginations what, or who, exists behind it. Instead, public perceptions about prisons and prisoners are shaped largely by media (mis)representations, including the grossly sensationalized genre of Hollywood prison films. On a recent visit to Cuba during which I interviewed three dozen women in prison, I was only half-surprised to learn that many of the women's preconceived notions about what prison would be like were based on portrayals they had seen in Hollywood films.

In the United States, where the prison industrial complex is expanding exponentially, the growth of the punishment industry occurs against the backdrop of a ubiquitous reluctance on the part of most people on the outside to engage in critical discussions about jails and prisons beyond the oversimplified and fatally inaccurate equation of prison expansion with the elimination of crime. Media and law enforcement agencies collude to create an increasingly crime-saturated atmosphere in which those who are least likely to be victims of crime are the very individuals most vocally supportive of harsher sentencing practices and prison expansion as means of curtailing crime. In the public imagination, fantastical notions of "the criminal" translate into fears of a (black male) stranger who lurks in dark corners waiting to beat, rob, rape, or murder an unsuspecting victim. The resulting "lock-'em-up-and-throw-away-the-key" attitude—exemplified at the legislative level by three- and, in some states, two-strikes laws—renders more and more invisible those who are imprisoned. The continued demonization of welfare mothers, particularly black single mothers, and the dismantling of programs that assist poor women and their children are carving out new gendered paths toward imprisonment.

This widespread invisibility of incarcerated populations, who tend to be conceptualized on a wholesale basis as the most loathsome offenders (invariably, attempts to raise discussions about alternatives to incarceration bring responses of "What about the murderers, rapists, and child molesters?") is profoundly exacerbated by gender; women prisoners are twice-marginalized, invisible in the "free" world by virtue of their incarceration, and largely overlooked even by prison activists by virtue of their gender. Statistics on who goes to prison tend to relate almost exclusively to men, since men make up the majority of the U.S. prison population. But the rate of increase in women's incarceration is almost twice the rate of increase for men. And while more and more prison activists are focusing on black men, numerically the most incarcerated population in U.S. society, what about black women, who represent the most rapidly increasing of all incarcerated populations?

Challenging the hyperinvisibility of women prisoners is central to effective activist and academic work around issues of imprisonment, and it guides the work of many people on the outside who provide a range of advocacy, aid, and support services to women in prison. As I looked again, this time more carefully, at the faces of the women represented in the photographs of *Behind the Razor Wire,* I wondered whether the distinctions I saw between them and the men portrayed in the book were a product of my own experiences as a formerly incarcerated woman and longtime prison activist or whether, in fact, the camera had captured reflections of the particular kind of invisibility, of social dispossession, to which women prisoners are subjected by virtue of the intersection of class, race, and gender. For me, Michael Jacobson-Hardy's invitation to contribute a foreword to this book marked an occasion for personal introspection in the context of my public work.

My interest in women's imprisonment—and my commitment as an activist to work for radical change in the U.S. penal system—dates back more than twenty-five years, when I was arrested and incarcerated. For sixteen months preceding my trial on charges of murder, kidnaping, and conspiracy, I was held in three jails—one in New York and two in California. My acquittal came in 1972, almost two years after my arrest, the result of a powerful international campaign that was organized around my case. That campaign literally saved my life. I will always be grateful to all of those—many of whom I never have had the opportunity to meet personally— who worked passionately and persistently as organizers and participants in that movement. Twenty-five years after my acquittal, I still harbor hopes of generating similar movements to free the one hundred political prisoners held in U.S. prisons and to shake the foundations of the criminal justice system, which has not only expanded its reach but has also become far more repressive and far more racist than we ever could have imagined.

I have not forgotten the sense of invisibility, isolation, and desolation I myself felt while I was locked up. This was due in large part to the fact that I was kept in solitary confinement for most of the time I spent in jail. But solitary confinement is hardly necessary to the production of feelings of remoteness during the experience of incarceration. Although a massive campaign was mounting on the outside around my case, during the earliest phases of my imprisonment the only way I learned of the movement was through my attorneys, family members, and members of the National United Committee to Free Angela Davis. Still, I am aware that I was far more visible, and far less isolated from the society from which I temporarily had been marginalized, than the vast majority of women and men in prison.

At the time of my imprisonment in New York, the Women's House of Detention, the first facility where I was held, was still located at the center of Greenwich Village. It was a living monument to an era when the invisibility of prison interiors was accentuated by their external ultravisibility. Years later I thought of the House of D. when I visited the vast panopticon prison at the center of the city of Breda in the Netherlands. In the New York jail, those of us on the inside were able to look down upon the "free" human activity in the streets below through the closely webbed metal grates that covered the windows of our cells. However, the "free" people in the streets, when they sought out the sources of the anonymous, disembodied voices emanating from this massive structure of brick and concrete, could see nothing, not even a vague silhouette.

Over twenty-five years later, people of my generation occasionally will tell me that they participated in street demonstrations outside the House of D., and that as they screamed "Free Angela Davis and all Political Prisoners" in unison with the other demonstrators, they tried in vain to detect the outlines of our faces behind the metal grating. Behind the walls and gates of the massive structure within which we were confined, we on the inside were invisible to the outside world. In contrast, the House of D. had an ominous and unmistakable—and indeed unavoidable—presence in the Village. It was not unlike a haunted house, a source of wonder and awe that might attract onlookers but that no one really wished to explore in depth. Many years prior to my arrest, as a high school student in Greenwich Village, I used to pass the House of D. on my way to the subway. I remember how I felt assaulted and frightened by the invisible voices gushing from that bizarre old building. I always quickened my pace in an attempt to shut them out. Little did I know then that one day mine would be among those invisible voices.

The one-sided public accessibility that characterized the House of D. at that time is certainly a thing of the past in the 1990s. Ironically, as U.S. prisons are proliferating more rapidly than ever before, and media and law enforcement agencies work in ever closer conjunction to create the image of a crime-saturated society that in turn perpetuates uncritical pro-prison attitudes, the very institutions that are seen as the end-all solution to the so-called crime problem—jails and prisons—become less and less visible from both an ideological and a geographical standpoint. The thoroughgoing remoteness of penal institutions enables the average citizen to feel safe, to imagine that "those people" are locked up somewhere far away, where they pose no threat to society. Even when these facilities are located within twenty minutes of major metropolitan areas, the ideological separation that is imposed on prisons and prisoners makes them seem a world away.

The economic and social factors that lead certain individuals to commit offenses that are likely to land them in prison—as well as the criminalization process itself, which dictates what segments of the population become the objects of the widespread fear of crime—go unaffected by the number of prisons that are built in the United States each year. Systemic social problems such as poverty, homelessness, illiteracy, and child abuse—each of which renders its victims more likely to become entangled in the penal system—require aggressive and innovative solutions that bear no relationship to incarceration. Yet these simple and rather obvious realities are obscure to most people who have not had some form of direct contact with the punishment industry. For this reason, it is vital that those of us who are active around prison issues promote as much firsthand exchange as possible between members of the "free" world and members of the imprisoned world. It is difficult to step inside a jail or prison, to talk with the people whose lives are confined to these facilities, without being deeply moved. Indeed, to hear the stories of incarcerated women and men is to recognize that little more than the luck of the draw—or, rather, of one's socioeconomic birthright—separates "us" from "them."

I count myself among those who work to create traffic between the outside and the inside. In the late 1980s I helped to design and began teaching an undergraduate course on incarcerated women at San Francisco State University. During the course of that class—which I co-taught or taught alone for several years and which is still offered at San Francisco State today—I was able to take the class into the San Francisco County Jail, where they engaged in discussions with prisoners. Sometime later, while still teaching the Incarcerated Women course at SFSU, I began simultaneously teaching a class on women's cultural awareness at the jail. With the agreement of both my students and the inmates, I incorporated into the agendas for the two classes weekly "field trips" during which a group of SFSU students accompanied me to the jail throughout the semester.

These exchanges between the students and prisoners were mutually beneficial on many levels, but without question it was the students who learned the most from the experience. What they discovered behind the gates and walls of this nearby yet remote correctional facility—which is entirely invisible except to those who know of its hidden location—was a world, and a population, about which many of them had little or no firsthand knowledge prior to enrolling in the course. Their subsequent work reflected a heightened level of critical inquiry into the questions raised by our readings and discussions about incarcerated women and the worlds they inhabit.

Every prison is a world unto itself, with a history as undiscovered as the institutions themselves. The Federal Correctional Institution in Pleasanton, California (FCI–Dublin) is just such a place, having opened in 1974 as a youth correctional facility and undergone several transformations since then. In 1977 it became an all-women's prison, and in 1980 a section was opened to house male prisoners who, for a variety of reasons—including open homosexuality and involvement in witness protection cases—are deemed ill-suited to traditional men's prisons.

At about the same time FCI–Dublin opened, I was settling in East Oakland after a long speaking tour that followed my acquittal. For almost twenty-five years I have lived very near this federal prison—which today houses a number of political prisoners, including several of the Puerto Rican women POWs—and though I have long been aware of its existence, for many years it loomed in my mind as a distant and remote place. That changed in 1996, when I made my first visit there in order to give a lecture to the women prisoners during Black History Month.

Driving to and from FCI–Dublin that February, I realized that the degree to which I felt physically removed from this particular prison was a function not of its actual distance from my East Oakland home—it is a mere twenty minutes away—but rather of the way its secluded geographical location works, in concert with the ideological construction of correctional institutions in general as far-flung repositories for malefactors, to create the illusion of inaccessibility. This illusion of inaccessibility works two ways: on the one hand, it is designed to persuade those on the outside that those who are locked away cannot reach into our homes, our neighborhoods, or, for that matter, our society; on the other hand, however, we in the "free" world rarely imagine ourselves being able to reach into the imprisoned world—that is, to enter into this world—without ourselves being arrested and imprisoned.

Since my first visit to FCI–Dublin in February 1996, I have returned twice. And each time my commitment as an activist is reinvigorated by my meetings with the very powerful women who are incarcerated there. I am also reminded, particularly as I savor my exchanges with the seven political prisoners who are confined there, that had it not been for the powerful movement for my freedom in the early seventies—and had I managed to evade the triple death penalty that was sought by the prosecutor who tried my case—today, twenty-seven years after my arrest, I probably still would be listed among the one hundred or so political prisoners currently being held in this country.

Alicia Rodriguez, her sister Ida Luz (Lucy) Rodriguez, Carmen Valentin, and Dylcia Pagan—all of whom are incarcerated in FCI–Dublin at this writing—are among the fifteen Puerto Rican activists presently serving what amount to life sentences on charges of seditious conspiracy, of attempting to overthrow the government of Puerto Rico. These four women were arrested on April 4, 1980. In October 1997, when I last visited FCI–Dublin, they had been imprisoned for over seventeen years. Alicia, who had recently been transferred to this facility, presently is serving a fifty-five-year federal sentence, on top of a thirty-year state sentence. Her sister Lucy has served an eight-year state sentence and presently is serving an eighty-year federal sentence. Carmen is serving a ninety-year sentence, and Dylcia, who also has served an eight-year state sentence, is, like Alicia, presently serving a fifty-five-year federal sentence.

The other three women political prisoners currently being held at FCI–Dublin are Linda Evans, Laura Whitehorn, and Marilyn Buck, all three of whom were arrested in 1985. Linda, Laura, and Marilyn are white women whose deep, long-term involvement in antiracist and anti-imperialist struggles made them the targets of severe repressive measures by the U.S. government. Their willingness to place themselves on the front lines of some of the more revolutionary movements in recent U.S. history landed them in prison; Linda is serving a forty-five-year sentence, Laura a twenty-year sentence, and Marilyn a total of seventy years.

The presence among the general population at FCI–Dublin of these political prisoners—whose commitments to social justice at every level have only been reinforced by their experiences of incarceration—has played an important role in politicizing the rest of the women there. During my October 1997 visit with them, I shared some of the findings of the research I had conducted in Cuban women's prisons the previous summer. The responses of the women as I described the positive aspects of the Cuban prison system—which is shaped in large part by its efforts to adhere to the United Nations Standard Minimum Rules for the Treatment of Prisoners (SMR)—revealed their frustration with the refusal of the U.S. penal system to do the same.

At the same time, however, the women at FCI–Dublin raised important questions about the contradictions that characterize the Cuban system. As I described the many ways women's relationships with their families—especially their children—are preserved through various aspects of the prison system in Cuba, Alicia pointed out that the presence of razor wire, which also surrounds prisons in Cuba, seems to contradict the country's efforts to diminish the physical barriers between free society and the imprisoned world. The guiding principle of the SMR—that individuals are sent to prison *as* punishment, not *for* punishment—is manifest in Cuban policies that permit families to have overnight visits in "family rooms" with their incarcerated relatives, and dictate that prison labor shall be compensated by the same wages that would be earned for similar work outside, but the Cuban system is far from perfect.

Yet juxtaposed with the U.S. system, Cuba may be seen as a model by which the treatment of prisoners in this country should be measured. Sentencing practices there limit the maximum term to twenty years, although with time off for good behavior and other incentive reductions, the average time served on a twenty-year sentence in Cuba is eight years. As I shared this sort of information with the women at FCI–Dublin, they asked how they could obtain copies of the SMR and were obviously impressed by Cuba's efforts to ensure the successful reintegration of prisoners into society upon their release.

My introduction to the interiors of the imprisoned world when I was arrested in 1970 was a horrifying ordeal during which I imagined on many occasions that I might never again resume my life on the outside. There were moments when I truly believed that I would become a casualty of the U.S. government—either by an "accident" that would leave me dead in the custody of law enforcement officials, or by the machinations of a judicial system that seemed poised to do away with me. Today my ability to move between the "free" world and the imprisoned world and act as a conduit between the inside and the outside—as well as between the closed worlds of different prisons, as was the case when I spoke about the Cuban penal system with women prisoners in FCI–Dublin—is not only an important part of my activism, but also a means of situating my personal experience of incarceration within the larger context of the need for radical changes in the U.S. prison system. It allows me to use my experience to work for those changes, and it is easily the most fulfilling work that I do.

If you are wondering what you can do, or what to tell others who want to know how they can help, begin by thinking and talking about imprisonment: who is at risk, who is affected, and why? Study the photographs in this book, and ask yourself whether you truly can imagine what life is like behind the razor wire. Who lives in the world portrayed here? What circumstances led these individuals to prison? How do their lives and the day-to-day conditions in which they live differ from the images you may have seen in Hollywood films or television programs dramatizing various aspects of the imprisoned world? If you do not have solid and complicated answers to these questions, perhaps you should consider becoming involved with an organization that does work around prisoners' rights. Perhaps you should think about visiting a correctional facility, or talking to someone who has been incarcerated. Think about going behind the razor wire. These photos are an important start.

Behind the Razor Wire

MICHAEL JACOBSON-HARDY

Male voices echoed against the cold cement walls of the three tiers of cells. "Hey picture man, take my picture. Hey motherfucker, get me out of this shit hole!" The volume of voices swelled as I stood, peering at the men inside the steel and concrete cages.

After several months of phone calling and letter writing, I had been permitted by the Suffolk County House of Correction in Boston to photograph the historic Deer Island jail in Winthrop. For more than two centuries Deer Island had been used to house society's "unwanted," immigrants and orphans, criminals and paupers. After King Philip's War (1675-76), "Native Americans were imprisoned on the island and sold into slavery in the West Indies. In the mid-19th century, Deer Island became an asylum for the city's social and economic outcasts" (Massachusetts Water Resources Authority, "History of Deer Island," 1991). In 1904 it once again became the site of a prison. The jail was about to be closed. My photographs were the last visual record of this ninety-year-old institution.

I arrived to find a small group of prison officials assembled in front of the administration building. We entered a narrow corridor under a sign reading "Pedestrian Trap." I passed through two metal detectors. My camera bags were inspected. I was asked if I was carrying any firearms. Had I ever committed a felony? I answered no and walked down a narrow, fenced-in passageway that led to the cellblocks. Lieutenant Jim Satori had been assigned to take me through the jail.

We passed a room where prisoners were held while they waited to be taken to court. Another room housed a wall of handcuffs and keys. We left the holding area and went back outside on our way to the maximum-security section of the jail. Our tour was interrupted by a frenzy of activity. Some guards communicated hurriedly over cellular phones while others sped back toward the holding room. A prisoner had become disruptive on his way back to jail and had splintered the wooden benches in the room. The commotion subsided. The prisoner was restrained and returned to his cell.

We entered the maximum-security building. Heavy steel bars enclosed three tiers of six-by-eight-foot cells. The bars were black and roughened with age. Some of them had been pried apart slightly. A spiral staircase stood in the far corner of the narrow walkway. A guard was stationed on the second tier. At first there was a deadening silence, interrupted only by an occasional prisoner's voice muttering obscenities. Many prisoners struck tough poses, perhaps to ward off a sense of powerlessness or to quell their fears. Some complained about poor conditions, overcrowding, and bad food.

I asked if I could go down onto the main floor and speak directly with the prisoners. The lieutenant warned that photographing from the floor might be risky. The men were apt to yell obscenities at me; some might spit at me or even urinate on me. I decided to take my chances. I asked one young black man if I could take his picture. He nodded in agreement, then stood motionless, his olive-drab prison suit unzipped to his waist, revealing a long scar on his stomach. Epithets ricocheted down the narrow corridor of concrete walls and barred windows. The group of prison officials assigned to take me through the jail became anxious to leave this section. The lieutenant motioned for me to move on. I made my last photograph and left the maximum-security section, the voices of the angry men fading into the distance.

In the medium-security cellblocks each cell was lit sparingly by a single bare bulb that hung from the ceiling. The floors were concrete. "I'll get out if I have to kill every screw in the joint" was scrawled on one wall. Stainless steel toilets had been installed in 1971. Prior to that, inmates used buckets, which they emptied each morning.

Gradually the prisoners returned and surrounded me while I photographed their cells. A young Puerto Rican man stood only a few feet away from me, gripping the cold steel bars of his cell. His body was in full view. I asked to make his portrait but the guard said no. The prisoner stared at me and I stared back into his hollow eyes. I felt somehow degraded in my freedom.

My visit to Deer Island was coming to an end. I went back through the "Pedestrian Trap" and came upon a group of black and Hispanic women and children who had come to visit their men inside. The oldest woman in the group gave me permission to photograph them. She stared with defiance into my camera.

I sat by the banks of Boston Harbor, a few hundred feet from the entrance to the jail. It was quiet now. Gentle waves lapped the shore. Seagulls circled nearby in search of food. But the desperate voices of the men inside maximum security reverberated in my mind.

The old Suffolk County House of Correction at Deer Island was slated for demolition. The prisoners were moved the following week to newer quarters in South Boston, where 55 percent of the 1,413 male inmates are black and 21 percent are Hispanic. All are poor. The old jail was torn down in preparation for the new Massachusetts Water Resources Authority sewage treatment plant—from human waste, to human waste the cycle continues at Deer Island.

From 1991 through 1996 I photographed inside several state prisons and county jails in Massachusetts. Massachusetts has a multilevel prison system consisting of state prisons and county jails. County jails like Deer Island incarcerate people for up to two and a half years; state prisons usually hold men and women for longer periods. Jail inmates are often young men who have committed less serious offenses. In recent years, however, the trend toward mixing serious and minor offenders has developed. With the high costs of building prisons and with fewer municipal funds available at the local level for jail construction, the state has gotten into the business of financing county jails. It costs from $50,000 to $100,000 to build a prison cell and another $29,604 per year to lock someone inside one. In order to get state money, county jails must agree to take state prisoners, who are often more violent and pose a threat to less dangerous inmates.

Deputy Superintendent Frank Godek at Hampshire County House of Correction in Northampton explained, "State prisoners tend to come from all over. They are shipped in from prisons in the Boston area because they pose a threat to the prison community there. They are often members of local gangs and know the other inmates in the Boston prisons. So the state sends them to western Massachusetts. We're mandated to take one hundred state prisoners." He added, "These inmates bring dangerous patterns from their cultures back home. You have more people coming in here and immediately arming themselves with home-made weapons." He opened his drawer and showed me a "shank" knife that was ground from a piece of hard plastic, an ice pick that was made from a sharpened nail with a wooden handle, and knives that had been fashioned from razor blades melted into toothbrush handles.

I received clearance from the Department of Corrections in Boston to photograph at the North Central Correctional Institution in Gardner, a medium-security state prison. Like Deer Island jail, NCCI had an unusual history. Before 1981 the prison had been used as a mental institution. The buildings were surrounded by two razor wire fences, with a high-voltage wire sandwiched between them. A dazed man, handcuffed and shackled, was being brought up the stone steps to the prison entrance as I approached.

Prisoners were allowed to wear their own clothing, which often consisted of blue jeans and sweatshirts. I was told to wear anything but jeans so that in case of a riot, I would be distinct from most prisoners.

Peter Chalapatis, who had worked at NCCI since it opened in 1981, was assigned to take me through the prison. Most of the men there were "lifers." They had done time in other, more secure state prisons and were deemed capable of living among upwards of forty inmates in prison dormitories. I found the men to be respectful of one another, for the most part. Mr.

Chalapatis, or P.J., as he was called by the men, explained, "I treat the men with respect and I expect the same." He told me that in many cases lifers are better behaved than those doing less time in county jails, where the men are usually younger and expect to be released sooner. Here the men understand that in some cases they will be living together for the rest of their lives and have to learn to get along.

Some of the men lay on their bunks, some watching small televisions attached to their bed frames. These TVs carried specially controlled prison programs. Not only TV fare, but other programs at the prison have been curtailed in recent years as the government has shifted its focus away from rehabilitation and toward retribution as a means of reducing crime.

It was noticeably quieter at NCCI than at Deer Island. I asked some inmates how they adjusted to this living situation, having come from prisons like the state maximum-security prison in Walpole where isolation in a six-by-eight-foot cell was the norm. "We had a guy who spent six years in isolation," Mr. Chalapatis said. "He couldn't make the adjustment to life here. We only take the ones who can adjust." Some called out to P.J., hoping to get him to respond to their requests. "My papers, did you get my papers?" cried one man. "When is my trial date?" asked another. I asked about prison overcrowding. "There are too many prisons being built," he said. "Many of the people in prison don't belong there. We shouldn't have men and women convicted on drug charges thrown in with murderers and rapists. These people should be out serving the community, perhaps in AIDS projects." He brought me back to the main gate, where I photographed the expanse of razor and high-voltage wire that vanished into the fog.

At MCI–Shirley, one of the newer medium-security state prisons, row upon row of faceless prison buildings loomed on the horizon. After the usual security checks I was taken into the living units in time for "count"—the daily routine of locking all the inmates in their cells and counting them. Some yelled back at the guards in protest, but they were finally locked down. This was the first time I had seen a female CO (correctional officer) in a men's prison.

I imagined she found it difficult when the men hurled obscenities at her. But she told me, "It's just a job. I try not to take it too personally." The cells were antiseptic. There were no pictures on the walls. I was surprised by how young the guards were. One of them remarked that prison jobs were among the most secure jobs in the country. "It's either this or the army," he said.

At the Charles Street Jail in Boston, festering toilets and corroded sinks hung from the dank cell walls. Many well-known prisoners, including Malcolm X, did time here. The jail had been the subject of numerous lawsuits and had finally been closed.

At MCI–Framingham, the nation's first women's prison (founded in 1879) women had once been incarcerated for adultery and other breaches of "public morality." I opened the heavy steel red doors at the entrance and approached a woman behind a glass window. I told her that I had a ten o'clock appointment. Lieutenant Virginia Land had been assigned to take me through the prison. I put all my belongings in a locker and passed through the metal detector. As we approached the main gate, a buzzer rang and two doors automatically opened and locked shut behind us. Lieutenant Land led me to the modular units, where it had been decided that I would photograph five women.

A large television blared in the distance. *The Price Is Right* held some of the women's attention. Some of them milled around in groups. Others did laundry. Each had a bunk and a foot locker with sheets and bedding. The lieutenant read the women's names aloud.

A black woman sat on her bunk and looked outside her barred window. I told her that she shouldn't feel obliged to smile for the camera. "I have no problem with that," she said. "I never smile. What's there to smile about in this place? I feel sad all the time." She stared into space and asked, "When do I get out of here?" One of the women suggested that I use a different camera angle. She told me that she would like to be a photographer someday.

Two white women posed next to each other for their portrait. The one on the left had the AIDS virus. "Got it using dirty needles," she said. She would probably spend the final days of her life in prison as a result of her own self-inflicted abuse. Both women were repeat offenders. One had been back to MCI–Framingham twelve times, the other ten. I left the modular unit and was taken to a more secure section of the prison, where newly admitted women were housed in padlocked cells. I asked the lieutenant what crimes these women had committed. She told me that most of the women were incarcerated for larceny, prostitution, using and selling drugs, armed robbery, and murder. Many have children who were in the care of relatives or court-appointed foster parents.

Dorothy Walsh, a prison volunteer who was working with the Alternatives to Violence program at MCI–Framingham, spoke with me about what she called the victim/perpetrator/victim cycle. She explained that many prisoners have been victims of child abuse. The economic and cultural deprivations that many of their families face are a breeding ground for abuse. Later on in life, these young victims become victimizers themselves. They lash out at others or hurt themselves, perhaps through drug abuse or prostitution. When they are brought to prison to be punished, they again become victims, and the cycle repeats itself. She believed that no one would hurt another human being if they had not previously been hurt themselves.

I photographed isolation units and prison cells that were no longer in use. I told the lieutenant that some of them reminded me of the ones I had seen at the Charles Street Jail in Boston. She paused and told me that she had worked there for three months. I asked if she believed that any real rehabilitation went on at MCI–Framingham. "No" was her reply.

I watched as women sewed American flags in the prison industries program. Some of them worked for fifty cents an hour, enough to buy cigarettes at the prison canteen. Across the street was the now closed General Motors plant. Its expansive parking lot was completely empty. The parking lot at MCI–Framingham, by contrast, was nearly full. The prison industry has become one of the largest growth industries in the United States, competing with education, health, and welfare for tax dollars.

Lieutenant Land greeted many of the women by name as we walked the grounds. "I get to know them," she said. "Many of these women are repeat offenders. They get out and, in six months or so, they're back. They may leave prison, but when they return they remember me. It's as if they never left."

I also photographed at the state's only maximum-security prison, formerly named MCI–Walpole. In the 1980s the residents of Walpole decided that they didn't want their city to be synonymous with the prison. They held a contest and changed the name to MCI–Cedar Junction, after a nearby abandoned railroad station.

The white concrete prison walls and shotgun towers rose up from a wooded area like a medieval fortress. In the main building I was given a copy of a media booklet and learned that the prison's electric chair had been destroyed by inmates in one of their many uprisings of the 1970s. From 1901 to 1947, sixty-five men had been electrocuted. No one had been executed since 1947, although the death penalty was not abolished until 1972. Those sentenced to death had their sentences commuted to life imprisonment. All of this could change, however, since Massachusetts governor William Weld, a former state prosecutor, has petitioned members of the legislature every year since his term began as governor in 1992 to reinstate the death penalty.

My tour began in the superintendent's office, where I was told what I could and could not photograph, and that in the event of a disturbance at the prison, no pictures could be taken. We toured the most notorious Departmental Segregation Unit in the prison, known as Ten Block. Allegations of prisoner abuse in this area have circulated among members of the general prison population for years.

In the multimillion-dollar Departmental Disciplinary Unit, first put to use in 1992, I photographed isolation units in which prisoners were deprived of sensory stimulation for long periods of time. The guard at the central control station watched them on a series of video monitors. The prisoners were locked behind heavy steel doors for twenty-three hours a day and allowed only occasional solitary exercise in the "kennels," cages enclosed by chain-link fences. Referring to poor recreation facilities, one prisoner cried out, "Show him the real yard. You spend millions of fuckin' dollars to hold us here and don't give us the shit that's legally ours."

Isolation in the segregation units is used as a tool by the guards to control and punish inmates. Those in the Departmental Disciplinary Unit can earn up to four visits from the outside per month by staying "disciplinary report" free, but in recent years all contact visits have been prohibited at the prison. Visits now take place behind glass walls and are monitored by guards.

Meanwhile, inside the prison industries building some men earned fifty cents an hour stamping license plates, manufacturing brooms, and ironing prison uniforms. I watched a man silk-screen the seal of the Commonwealth of Massachusetts.

Public Information Officer Richard McCarthy at the Hampden County House of Correction arranged for me to photograph at the York Street jail in Springfield. As we neared the cellblocks, he showed me a mark on the floor near the gate where prisoners had once been hanged, a bleak reminder of the jail's long history.

We entered the main cellblock and walked the length of the corridor looking for inmates to photograph. Light streamed into the cellblock from large barred windows on the east side of the building. Prisoners lay wrapped in blankets, resting in their cells. There was a constant drone of prison noise as cell doors opened and slammed shut. The men were allowed to move freely at this hour of the morning. A group of Hispanic men was sweeping the stairs leading to the second tier. It reminded me in some ways of a military barracks. Some of the tough guys popped off at each other, trying to stay afloat in the dark waters of prison life. The blanket-wrapped figures in the cells made me think of body bags. I thought about the large numbers of men and women warehoused in prisons, the tremendous cost in human lives and resources. Given better circumstances and choices, these men and women may have been able to lead productive lives.

As I turned to leave the cellblock I came upon a white prisoner. Withered and forlorn, he looked away and would not respond to the guards who tried to make contact with him. I entered the jail library and observed men learning basic skills; some practiced simple math calculations. Others stumbled over words as they tried to read aloud. Most could not read or write. A crucifix hung from the wall; the library also served as a church.

The York Street jail in Springfield was closed later that year. The inmates were transferred to the new twelve-hundred-bed facility in Ludlow, which I photographed in 1994. The high-tech $75 million concrete, steel, and glass fortress, the envy of any public education system in the country, was built on a swamp. Today's high-tech prisons are no longer built with bars. These have been replaced by heavy steel doors and narrow window slits. The drone of prison voices is no longer heard in these units, since inmates are locked in soundproof enclosures for longer periods of time. Prison psychologists report seeing more and more inmates with symptoms of paranoia caused by lengthy stays in these new enclosures. The transition from the old jail to this new, high-tech prison was difficult for many of the inmates, who were also forbidden to smoke. The place was completely sterile. No pictures were allowed on the walls. The adjustment was so hard that during the initial move from the York Street jail, some of the inmates had even tried to get relocated to the maximum-security prison in Walpole, claiming that the new antiseptic facility was driving them crazy.

I asked Mr. Richard McCarthy about the demographics of the prison population. "The vast majority of inmates," he said, "have never lived in a household with an income defined as middle-class. The minority population is disproportionately represented, as it is in prisons everywhere. Hampden County House of Correction has upwards of 40 percent Hispanic, 30 percent African American. At any given time the Caucasian-Anglo population is about 20 percent, an exact reversal of the community at large." He told me that he had visited Riker's Island in New York, where "the minority population is even greater: of fifteen-thousand inmates, upwards of 95 percent are minority." In its most recent annual survey of jails, the U.S. Department of Justice reported that in 1994 the incarceration rate among blacks was almost six times that of whites. Sixty-five percent of prison inmates belonged to racial or ethnic minorities in 1991, up from 60 percent in 1986 (U.S. Department of Justice, Survey of State Prison Inmates, 1991).

Ruth Connors, the substance abuse educator and program planner for the Hampden County Sheriff's Department, told me that most inmates have been traumatized in childhood by neglect, physical abuse, and mental abuse. She explained that individuals who don't get nurturing when they need it become "shame-based" people, and if they hurt, they hurt others. Most of them are poor. "The new crime bill isn't going to do anything," she said. "We need prevention. We have to support families. We have to keep kids in school. We have to have adults around who children can relate to, who they can trust and have as a role model. The more money you put into prevention, the better off you are going to be."

In response to growing public pressure, fed by fears of violent crime, state governments are building more prisons. In 1995 Massachusetts governor William Weld petitioned members of the state legislature to pass a $705 million bond issue to build five thousand new prison cells. In an effort to dramatize his political agenda, he airlifted 299 of the state's least dangerous inmates to a Dallas, Texas, jail. State prison officials claimed that the airlift was done to ease prison and jail overcrowding. In February 1996, the Massachusetts legislature passed a smaller $483 million bond bill to construct and repair several prisons and jails in the commonwealth. A disappointed Governor Weld chastised members of the legislature over the reduced bond bill, claiming that "the Legislature didn't want to charge into the future."

Prisons in Massachusetts continue to be overcrowded and are currently operating at 150 percent of capacity. A 1994 Massachusetts House of Representatives study concluded that "The [governor's] construction program [alone] could cost the Commonwealth $150 million annually and a billion dollars over the life of the bonds, and would not reduce overcrowding." No matter how many new prisons are built, the fact is that every cell in them will be filled. New tough laws, including mandatory minimums and stringent antidrug laws, have flooded our prisons. Increasingly they have become warehouses for people of color and victims of poverty, alienation, and abuse.

It is estimated that over the next ten years, taxpayers will pay $450 million to run the new $75 million Hampden County House of Correction in Ludlow. An official at the jail told me that in ten years, prison spending will probably bankrupt the state. Is this how we as a society should be allocating our precious resources? We seem to have replaced the ideal of rehabilitation with the harsh logic of retribution. Does this promise to resolve the problem or does it in fact contribute to it? Should we instead be focusing our attention on the sources of crime, on eliminating racism, poverty, neglect, and abuse?

I asked my probation officer friend what he thought was the solution to the crisis in corrections today. He pointed to his two-year-old son and said, "Take care of them when they're little." George Counter, former superintendent of the Holyoke Public Schools, one of the poorest school districts in Massachusetts, told me, "It cost $75 million to build the jail in Ludlow. It costs only $12,000 a year to pay for a Head Start teacher. So you can pay me now—or pay me later."

Doing Time, Marking Race

JOHN EDGAR WIDEMAN

P risons do their dirtiest work in the dark. The evil they perpetrate depends on a kind of willed ignorance on the part of the public. To prevent the worst abuses and realign our prison system with enlightened notions of justice and rehabilitation as well as punishment, the public must play an active role: awareness of what happens behind the walls is a crucial first step.

Art can be a means of redressing the public's ignorance and wishful thinking about prisons. The truth of art—in a book of photos, a story, poems, autobiography, dance, a movie—can throw light on what occurs inside prisons. This light, whether a source of revelation for millions, a spur to political reform, or simply one more candle burning, will help to dispel the nightmare we've allowed our prisons to become.

I know far too much about prisons. More than I ever wished to know. From every category of male relative I can name—grandfather, father, son, brother, uncle, nephew, cousin, in-law—at least one member of my family has been incarcerated. I've researched the genesis of prisons, visited prisons, taught in prisons, written about them, spent a night here and there as a prisoner. Finally, I am a descendant of a special class of immigrants—Africans—for whom arrival in America was a life sentence in the prison of slavery. None of the above is cited because it makes me proud or happy, but I feel I should identify some of the baggage, whether bias or insight, I bring to a discussion of prisons.

The facile notion of incarceration (read apartheid) as a cure for social, economic, and political problems has usurped the current national discussion. *Which candidate is tougher on crime* was the dominant issue dramatized in TV ads during the last election campaign. And the beat goes on.

"Tougher" seems to mean which candidate behaves more like the bullies I encountered in junior high school, the guys with fierce looks, macho words and posturing, who lorded it over the weakest kids, stealing their lunch money, terrorizing and tormenting them to gain a tough-dude image. Cowards at the core, bad actors mimicking the imagined thugs who keep them awake at night.

What bothered me most about the hysterical, bloodthirsty TV ads during the last election was the absolute certainty of the candidates that the prison cells they promised to construct, the draconian prison terms and prison conditions they would impose if elected, would never confine them or those who voted for them. Ignorance, racism, naiveté couldn't account for this arrogant, finger-pointing certainty. The only way they could be so sure was to know the deck was stacked, know that they enjoyed an immunity. The ones they were promising to lock up and punish, by design, would never be their people. Always somebody else. Somebody other. Not their kind. The fix was in. Without referring explicitly to race or class, the candidates and their audiences understood precisely who the bad guys would continue to be, once the candidates assumed power. I recall a sentencing hearing in a courtroom, the angry father (white) of a victim urging a judge (white) to impose upon a young man (black), who'd pleaded guilty, the most severe punishment because "they're not like us, Your Honor."

Honest fear, thoughtful perplexity, a leavening of doubt or hesitancy, the slightest hint, then or now, that what the candidates insinuated about the "other," about criminals and misfits, also implicated them would be a welcome relief. Instead the rhetoric continues, Manichean, divisive, and absolute, the forces of light doing battle with the forces of darkness.

As an African American, as a human being, I haven't yet shaken the sense of being personally assaulted by the campaign appeals to the electorate's meanest instincts. Nor have I been able to forgive the success of the tactic.

Sure enough, our country's in deep trouble. Drastic measures are required. But who says we must always begin at the bottom, taking from those who have least? Why heap more punishment on the losers, the tiny minority of lawbreakers who are dumb or unlucky enough to get caught and convicted? Building more prisons doesn't decrease crime. Removing federal money from some citizens' hands (the poor) and placing it in others' (the rich) doesn't save the nation billions. Why are patently false cures proclaimed and believed with such passionate conviction?

Why not start at the top? Limit maximum income. Reduce military spending. Wouldn't it be better to be swept from the earth while trying to construct a just society, rather than holding on, holding on, in a fortress erected to preserve unfair privilege? What indefensible attitudes are we assuming toward the least fortunate in our society? Isn't shame the reason we are desperately intent on concealing from ourselves the simple injustice of our actions?

We're compiling a hit list. Retrogressing. Deciding once more it's in the nation's interest to treat some as more equal than others. Belief that America is burdened by incorrigibles—criminals, the poor and untrained, immigrants too different to ever fit in—is an invitation to political leaders who can assure us they have the stomach and clean hands to dispose of surplus people pulling the rest of us down. We're looking to cold-eyed, white-coated technocrats and bottom-line bureaucrats for efficient final solutions. If this sounds paranoid or cartoonish, you must be unaware of facilities such as the Departmental Disciplinary Unit sensory deprivation cells at Massachusetts Correctional Institution–Cedar Junction, where prisoners are locked up twenty-three hours a day: chilling, high-tech, supermax prisons driving their inmates to madness and worse.

The sad, defeatist work of building prisons, the notion that prison walls will protect us from crime and chaos are symptomatic of our shortsightedness, our fear of engaging at the root, at the level that demands personal risk and transformation, our fear of confronting the real problems caging us all.

In the guise of outrage at crime and criminals, hard-core racism (though it never left us) is making a strong, loud comeback. It's respectable to tar and feather criminals, to advocate locking them up and throwing away the key. It's not racist to be against crime, even though the archetypal criminal in the media and the public imagination almost always wears "Willie" Horton's face. Gradually, "urban" and "ghetto" have become code words for terrible places where only blacks reside. Prison is rapidly being re-lexified in the same segregated fashion.

For many, the disproportionate number of blacks in prison is not a worrisome issue; the statistics simply fulfill racist prophecy and embody a rational solution to the problem of crime. Powerful evidence, however, suggests that racism may condition and thereby determine where the war on drugs is waged most vigorously. A study summarized in the *New York Times* on October 5, 1995, indicates that although African Americans represent about 13 percent of the total population and 13 percent of those who are monthly drug users, they are 35 percent of those arrested for drug possession, 55 percent of those convicted for possession, and 74 percent of the total serving sentences for possession.

We seem doomed to repeat our history. During the nineteenth century institutions such as prisons, orphanages, asylums, and poorhouses developed as instruments of public policy to repair the gaping rents in America's social fabric caused by rapid industrialization and urbanization. Politicians driven by self-interest, hoping to woo businessmen and voters with a quick fix, avoided confrontation with the underlying causes of social instability and blamed the poor. Inborn idleness, irresponsibility, uncontrollable brutish instincts, inferior intelligence, childlike dependence were attributed to the lower classes. Public policies, focusing on this incorrigible otherness, defined the state's role as custodial, separating and controlling suspect populations. State intervention into the lives of the poor neither diminished crime nor alleviated misery, but did promote fear and loathing of the victims of chaotic social upheaval.

Today young black men are perceived as the primary agents of social pathology and instability. The cure of more prisons and longer prison terms is being applied to them. They will be the ones confined, stigmatized, scapegoated. Already squeezed out of jobs, education, stable families, and communities, they are increasingly at risk as more and more of the street culture they have created, under incredible stress to provide a means of survival, is being criminalized (and callously commercialized). To be a man of color of a certain economic class and milieu is equivalent in the public eye to being a criminal.

Prison itself, with its unacceptably large percentage of men and women of color, is being transformed by the street values and street needs of a younger generation of prisoners to mirror the conditions of urban war zones and accommodate a fluid population who know their lives will involve inevitable shuttling between prison and the street. Gang affiliation, drug dealing, the dictates of gang leaders have replaced the traditional mechanisms that once socialized inmates. Respect for older, wiser heads, the humbling, sobering rites of initiation into a stable prison hierarchy have lost their power to reinforce the scanty official impetus toward rehabilitation that prison offers. The prison is the street, the street is prison.

If we expand our notion of prison to include the total institution of poverty, enlarge it to embrace metaphorical fetters such as glass ceilings that limit upward mobility for executives of color, two facts become apparent: There is a persistence of racialized thinking that contradicts lip service to a free, democratic society; and for people of color, doing time is only one among many forms of imprisonment legitimized by the concept of race.

Two Hundred Years of the Penitentiary
A National Infatuation with Incarceration

MARC MAUER

Two hundred years ago Quakers and other reformers in Pennsylvania conceptualized a new institution to respond to crime problems of the day. In keeping with their belief that crimes were committed by sinners who required an environment in which to be penitent, the new institution was termed the "penitentiary."

Prior to this, the American colonists had relied on a combination of physical, often brutal punishments for crime, along with public shaming and isolation from the community. As we can recall from depictions of that time, punishment by flogging, use of the stocks, and resort to the death penalty were quite common for a range of offenses. Banishment from the community was also employed as a means of expressing the society's condemnation of the offender.

The invention of the penitentiary, therefore, was a break with the past. With religious reformers in the lead, the new institution held out the promise of reforming sinners and enabling them to resume a law-abiding role in the community. This was to be accomplished through Bible study and contemplation, generally under conditions of solitary confinement. Competing models of prison systems were soon established in New York and other states, emphasizing discipline and order under a system of labor performed in silence.

The gap between theory and reality, unfortunately, proved to be rather wide. The isolation of the prisoners, from other inmates as well as from the outside world, not only hindered their rehabilitation but in many cases arguably caused greater harm. Little crime control impact on the larger community could be documented.

In the intervening two hundred years we have seen different philosophies competing for primacy as the stated goals of the prison system. Thus, while rehabilitation gained favor after World War II, the national conservative tide emerging in the 1970s has since led to the promotion of punishment as the overriding goal of the system.

The irony of this shifting of rationales is that the institution itself has hardly changed in the process. One day the prison cell is designed to make the inmate a better person; the next day it's function is to punish the inmate for his or her wrongs. This is not to overlook significant differences among prisons—between well-run institutions and violence-laden ones, or between chain gangs and treatment programs. But the basic structure of the prison— keeping people in cages (or in some newer institutions, in locked rooms) surrounded by high walls with armed guards—has changed remarkably little over time.

As we look at Michael Jacobson-Hardy's photographs, what emerges most clearly are the faces of the people locked behind bars. All one needs to do to place this in context is to look at a local newspaper and read a day's crime stories or political proposals on crime, and then to look back at the people in prison. We can then ask ourselves how the bars, steel, and cages in the photos respond to the crime problems we read about. Or, for the particular inmate at whom we gaze, what do we know about how he or she came to be locked up in the prison, and what is it about the prison that we expect will somehow speak to those factors?

There will be immediate objections to these questions, of course. What about the victims? Who cares about these criminals? Haven't they earned their punishment? But just a moment's reflection on these political sound bites shows how shallow they are. Who among us has not been victimized by crime, or had close friends or loved ones who have been? Who among us has not altered his or her lifestyle in part because of perceptions of "safe neighborhoods"? And how many among us have led an entirely crime-free life, with no youthful shoplifting experiences and no illegal alcohol or drug consumption?

So the attempted division of the nation into two camps—victims and offenders—paints an unrealistically uniform picture of good and evil. More important, it does little to help us resolve any of these very troubling problems. Why, after all, can't one be concerned about both the harm that is done to victims and the harm that is perpetrated on those in prison? The history of prison reformers, ranging from the early Quakers to more modern activists, has in fact rarely involved calls for merely turning open the prison gates. Rather, the concern of reformers has been to reduce the dehumanization of the prisoner and in the process, to create a safer community.

Even the idea of reforming the prison, though, virtually accepts the validity of the prison cell as a reasonable response to the crime problem, so much so that it becomes difficult in either political discourse or everyday problem solving to imagine other solutions. This remains our popular image, though with one important qualification. We actually look to prison primarily as the solution for just one part of the crime problem—young urban males who commit "street crimes."

For other groups of offenders, our first reaction is not necessarily to think of incarceration. White-collar offenders who knowingly pollute the environment or deliberately violate health and safety laws are not the images that come to mind when we think of "criminals." Nor are otherwise law-abiding middle-class citizens who seem to break the law in great numbers every year on April 15 when they file income taxes with a bit of touching up here and there. When an audit actually detects some of this creative accounting, the systemic response is generally not a criminal justice one, but rather an administrative punishment—payment of the delinquent taxes, plus a penalty.

In fact, the closer we get to home, the less clear it becomes that prison is the preferred solution to our problems. When one of our children starts abusing drugs, it does not occur to most of us to write out a check for $20,000 and turn him or her over to the local prison system. Instead we seek the best treatment program we can find and bring a variety of resources to bear on the problem. Others in society may not be so fortunate as to have health insurance or access to high-quality treatment, and so it is for them that we reserve mandatory sentences, prison cells, and bleak futures.

We focus on the prison because it is the most visible and symbolic aspect of our national response to crime, but in fact our national infatuation with both incarceration and the criminal justice system has led us greatly astray in our understanding of the problem at hand. Thus we see a quintupling of the number of people locked up in prison over the past twenty-five years, and we can't understand why this has apparently had so little impact on crime. Common sense would suggest that crime rates should have plummeted with a million additional inmates behind bars. In this case, though, common sense turns out to be wrong.

The main problem with this reasoning is that both prison and the entire criminal justice apparatus are after-the-fact responses to crime. Since half of all serious crimes are never even reported to the police and only about one-tenth actually result in an arrest, the criminal justice system at its best is responding only to a small fraction of the offending population.

The problem is aggravated by the fact that crime is disproportionately a young man's game. Across all racial and class lines, males in their late teens commit crimes at far higher rates than other demographic groups. So while we achieve some modest amount of crime reduction by incapacitating large numbers of offenders, each year brings a new cohort of potential offenders into the high crime rate years. Compounding this problem is the fact that teenagers are notorious for displaying a short time horizon; the threat of punishment in the future is not often foremost in their minds. The challenge, therefore, is to explore whether various interventions can aid in reducing the absolute level of crime committed during these years.

Despite the fact that the United States has now become a world leader in incarceration, apparently this is still not enough to satisfy certain political needs. We now hear talk of the coming generation of "superpredators," young urban males who will be growing in numbers and dangerousness over the next decade or so. One wonders whether a similar phenomenon is expected in Canada, Japan, or Sweden. Or whether this situation might have something to do with the deadly combination of drugs, guns, and poverty. Or, finally, whether the racial and economic status of these young offenders might have something to do with our apparent reluctance to conceive of more innovative approaches to the problem.

Prison reformers have come and gone, as have our differing notions of the goals of the system. In its most recent incarnation, the prison reform movement of the 1960s brought together a significant number of inmates, Black Muslims, antiwar activists, and others to mount a challenge to conditions of confinement in prisons as well as to the nature of justice as dispensed by the criminal justice system. Thus our attention was directed both to institutions that violated any sense of common decency and to the often arbitrary nature of sentencing and paroling policies.

Almost as quickly as this movement formed, however, it largely died out, leaving just pockets of reformers at the margins of the public policy debate. This demise can be traced to broader changes in the political and economic climate of the country over the past twenty years. These have affected the prospects not only for prison reform, but for humane social policy changes generally. Thus the scapegoating of prisoners that has emerged in recent years is very much parallel to similar attitudes toward welfare mothers, immigrants, and other groups at the bottom of the ladder. A wry commentary on these issues is offered by the chorus to a recent song wherein a confused average American realizes the source of all his problems—"it's teenage immigrant welfare mothers on drugs."

The broader context for these attitudinal shifts is the economic and social changes that the nation has undergone in the past fifty years. Following World War II and lasting for about twenty-five years was a period marked by an expanding economy, a world leadership role for the United States, and a sense of optimism for the future, at least among the majority population.

Beginning in the 1970s, though, the country was wrenched by national and global economic changes—the energy crisis, the decline of the manufacturing economy, and the growing disparity in wealth between the rich and the poor. The expanding economic pie of the first period offered at least the hope of a larger share for all. The contraction that followed set up a competition for limited resources, and a climate that was not conducive to promoting a caring community. The heightening of racial tensions that ensued may not have been inevitable, but it was certainly not surprising.

Thus, two hundred years after the birth of the penitentiary, we find ourselves in a difficult state of affairs: a prison population that has been bursting out of control for two decades with no end in sight, a hardening of attitudes toward prisoners, heightened racial tensions, and an economic climate that is not conducive to compassion for others. Is there any hope for the development of more rational policy and more humane responses?

Some glimmers of hope are present, but it is difficult to predict what coalescence of forces will bring about change. Within the corrections establishment itself, voices of reason and moderation have been increasingly heard in recent years. As prison wardens, police chiefs, and others recognize that they alone cannot solve the crime problem, they have been speaking out with more authority about the need for a more balanced approach to these problems.

The fiscal impact of current policies is at long last beginning to receive attention among policy makers. As the cost of incarceration threatens the viability of public education and other vital services, community leaders are questioning the trade-off in resources and the implications for the future.

If change is to come, it will also need to develop from grassroots pressure. For every politician who contends that he is "tough on crime" because his constituents demand it, there needs to be a vocal constituency advocating for services for both victims and offenders as well as an end to political rhetoric that obscures meaningful debate.

Ultimately any movement for change will in large part be based on the degree to which we can humanize and individualize the offenders going through the system. The more we can identify these people as young adults with problems rather than just nameless and faceless "criminals," the greater the prospects for thinking about more creative ways to respond to their behaviors. It is probably too much to hope that we can have substantial numbers of people visit prisons and develop a feel for the men and women who are locked up, but gazing at their photographs through a collection like this at least begins to provide us with a sense of the complexity of these human beings. Once we have begun that process, we are moving in the right direction.

Marc Mauer

Two Hundred Years of the Penitentiary

Pictures of Pain

The Criminality of the Criminal Justice System

JAMES GILLIGAN, M.D.

What could one possibly say about the pictures in this book that the photographs themselves have not already conveyed, more vividly than any words can? What words could describe the filth and sordidness of the toilet photographed at Deer Island? The animalizing effect of the "kennels" in which living human beings—or should I call them the living dead?—are caged at Walpole for what the state calls "recreation" (a euphemism so cynical that it would be laughable if it were not so cruel)? The claustrophobic atmosphere of the solitary confinement cells in which hundreds of still-living human beings are buried alive in every prison and jail in this state and this country, so that even if their bodies survive, their souls will die—while we congratulate ourselves for being "humane," since we are killing only the soul and not the body? The soul-murdering poverty and sterility of the iron and concrete cages that all prisoners are locked in, which have been deliberately stripped even of the pathetically few personal belongings these men, women, and children had previously used to support their already fragile, because damaged, sense of personal identity, personhood, indeed humanity?

So many misconceptions and egregiously inaccurate stereotypes about prisons circulate in what passes for public debate in this country that I hardly know where to begin in my effort to answer the questions I have just raised. I will start, nevertheless, with the disturbing observation that neither words nor pictures, no matter how vivid, can do more than give a faint suggestion of the horror, brutalization, and degradation of the prisons of this country. I speak from extensive personal knowledge of this subject, for I have spent twenty-five years of my professional life behind bars—not as an inmate, but as a prison psychiatrist. And I know from repeated, daily observation that neither pictures nor words alone can convey the stench that assaults the nostrils the moment one walks into these charnel houses of the spirit. Nor the hellish heat that oppresses you so pitilessly in the depth of the summer even in the more comfortable sections of this enclosed pressure cooker that it is not at all surprising that prisoners literally die from heatstroke from time to time, if they have the misfortune to live in the top tiers of the grotesquely misnamed "maximum-security" wing. Nor the reflexive spasm of dread that shakes your shoulders when a whole series of massive cast-iron doors crash and clang shut behind you as you enter deeper and deeper into the bowels of the prison, startling you no matter how often you have heard them and regardless of how firmly you know they will do the same thing again, so loudly do they hammer on your hearing, to the point that your ears are still ringing so loudly a half hour later that it is difficult to register the human speech with which desperate and lonely prisoners struggle to gain your attention so you can help them overcome their own confusion.

Pictures reach only your sense of sight, and words your mind; but when you are actually inside a prison, one overpowering and unmistakable message is repeatedly slammed into all of your five senses, through the symbolism of sadism by which these theaters of cruelty express the thought that this whole ghastly and inhuman underworld embodies in every atom of its nonbeing: HERE LOVE IS DEAD. And if God is Love, we do not need Nietzsche to inform us that God is dead also; nor do we need the Evangelists to remind us that the individuals who killed Him were ordinary, well-meaning people exactly like us, operating through the established legal authorities just as we do today. Crucifixion was, after all, merely the method of capital punishment utilized by the "criminal justice" system of its day (an ironically apt illustration of how literally if unconsciously accurate the name of that system is, given how easily and frequently "justice" itself *becomes* "criminal"; as Freud said, self-betrayal leaks out of every pore).

Now I realize that the piety of some believers might be offended by any comparison between Christ and criminals; the whole point of the Christian story, after all, is that that was precisely the mistake the Romans made—to treat Christ, a man "without sin," as if he were morally identical to the criminals who were crucified next to him. And whatever else one can say about the criminals who fill our prisons today, none of them are without sin (not that the rest of us are either, though that uncomfortable fact tends to be minimized by those who are eager to make prisons as cruel as possible).

Nevertheless, we will not advance the public policy debate about criminal violence in this country if we deny or minimize the terrible fact that some of the inmates in our prisons—a minority, but an extremely important one—are there because they themselves treated other people with a degree of cruelty that is indeed appalling, that no society can or should permit or tolerate, and that no government should allow its citizens to be subjected to (to the extent that governments can prevent it from happening). I have known far too many men whose behavior has made it impossible for us to engage in simplistic or naive responses to violent crime; these men cannot be allowed to live among the rest of us, at least for the foreseeable future. So when I say that prisons and punishment cause far more violence than they prevent, I of course do not mean that we should let murderers and rapists roam our streets (as if that were the only alternative to our present system of dealing with violent crime).

I am a physician, and I see violence (whether it is legal or illegal, homicidal or suicidal, intentional or careless) as a public health problem—indeed, the most important and dangerous threat to public health in our time. Because it affects mostly the young, violence kills more people below the age of sixty-five in this country than the two illnesses that are often (and mistakenly) thought to be the major causes of death, cancer and heart disease, combined. So I cannot emphasize too strongly how seriously I take the problem of violence. Far from being tolerant or permissive toward it, I am far more strongly opposed to violence in all its forms and in all its legal statuses, and far less tolerant and permissive toward it than are those who believe that our salvation lies in building more and more punitive (i.e., violent) prisons, and in responding to the violence called "crime" with more violence of our own (called "punishment").

But we need to make several important distinctions here if we are going to be able to think clearly about the problem of crime and violence. We need to distinguish between *crime* and *violence*; between *punishment* and *restraint*; and between the *punishment*, as opposed to the *prevention*, of violent behavior.

The moment we make the first of those distinctions, we notice that the usual tendency to use the words "crime" and "violence" as if they were interchangeable or synonymous is extremely misleading, for *most crime is not violent* and *most violence is not criminal*. Most of the crimes that are committed are nonviolent property crimes, nonviolent drug law violations, nonviolent violations of certain definitions of "morality," such as prostitution and gambling, and so on. We shoot ourselves in the foot when we send people to prison for nonviolent crimes, for there is no surer way to turn a nonviolent person into a violent one; and yet we have been sending a higher and higher proportion of people to prison in this country for nonviolent crimes over the past twenty years.

And most violence is not criminal. That is, most of the violent (nonnatural) deaths that occur are caused by behaviors that are perfectly legal. For example, far more people die from suicide than from criminal homicide, in this country and every other developed nation. Warfare (an activity that not only is legal, but that it can be illegal *not* to participate in) kills far more people than murder does. Indeed, activities such as foolish risk-taking behaviors, sheer carelessness, reckless driving, machismo, bravado, proving one's courage and "manhood" by engaging in dangerous sports, and exposing one's employees to hazardous working conditions collectively kill three to four times as many people each year in this country as are killed by all those whom we call murderers. There is even compelling evidence, from the University of California Medical School, that as many as fifty thousand nonsmokers a year die from the effects of "secondhand" tobacco smoke; that is twice as many people as are killed by those whom we call murderers. Yet smoking is perfectly legal, and nobody would think of punishing it by sending smokers to prison.

None of this is meant to minimize in the least the ineffaceable human suffering that is caused by those homicides that we happen to label "criminal"; it is merely to put those deaths in perspective, and to suggest that from a public health perspective, the criminal homicides—over which presidential elections are won or lost, and for the ostensible sake of which we are bankrupting ourselves by building and filling far more prison cells than any other country on earth, including those we call "police states"—are a tiny fraction of the violent deaths (the humanly caused lethal injuries) that we do not happen to label "criminal" and therefore do not punish.

It is also important not to confuse restraint with punishment. By *restraint* I mean preventing violence by physically depriving people of the freedom of movement with which they could inflict injuries—i.e., violence—on anyone (themselves or others), when voluntary means of preventing violence have not succeeded, and without inflicting pain or injury on the person being restrained. Coming between two children who are fighting, holding the arms of a child who is assaulting someone, holding a child so he will not run into traffic, temporarily placing a child in his room until he is able to control his temper and avoid assaulting anyone would all be examples of restraint (as opposed to punishment). Hitting or slapping the child, on the other hand, deliberately hurting him, twisting or breaking his arm, or assaulting him in any way after he has already been restrained and is no longer dangerous to himself or others would be examples of what I mean by punishment.

Adults were often restrained, or quarantined, in the past when they suffered from communicable diseases for which effective treatments and preventions did not yet exist (e.g., Typhoid Mary, sufferers from tuberculosis or scarlet fever, etc.). In the present day, people who are seriously mentally ill sometimes need to be restrained in order to prevent self-mutilation, suicide, assault, or homicide—but only when all other attempts to induce voluntary self-control or to achieve the primary prevention of violent behavior have failed, only for as long as they are demonstrably dangerous to themselves or others, and only under conditions that are as humane and respectful, rather than as punitive and degrading, as is humanly possible.

Punishment is the opposite of restraint. The word comes from *poine* and *poena*, the Greek and Latin words for *revenge*; they are also the roots of our word *pain*. Just as restraint means the *prevention* of violence, *punishment* means the deliberate and gratuitous *infliction* of violence (emotional or physical pain or injury) on someone, above and beyond any that is unavoidably and unintentionally inflicted in the process of restraining him. Punishment in this sense is one of the main purposes of the prison system. The current governor of Massachusetts, William Weld, was elected to office on the campaign promise to "reintroduce prisoners to the joys of busting rocks." Several southern states reintroduced chain gangs to their prison systems. And as is pointed out elsewhere in this book, Massachusetts prison authorities openly acknowledge that the deliberate purpose of the solitary confinement unit of their maximum-security prison is "punishment."

Since those same authorities claim that the purpose of punishing an inmate in this way is *deterrence*—that is, to deter him and others from committing further infractions of prison regulations in the future—it is worth distinguishing between *punishment* and *prevention*. Punishment is the deliberate infliction of pain on someone *after* he has victimized someone else, that is, after violence has already occurred and there is already a victim. Prevention, by contrast, is the process of eradicating or neutralizing the *causes* of violent behavior *before* it has occurred, so that there is no victim, and there is no violence to punish. Placing the emphasis on punishing violent offenders *after* they have created victims (as we have increasingly done in this country), rather than engaging in the primary prevention of violence *before* it has occurred (of which we are doing less and less in this country), is tantamount to locking the barn door after the horse is stolen—or rather, after the victim is killed. Our emphasis on punishment reveals the fact that we have become more interested in the perpetrators of violent crime than we are in the victims; for we are spending incomparably more of our limited resources on being punitive toward the perpetrators than we are on protecting the victims by preventing their victimization in the first place.

There is a widespread misimpression that punishment deters violence—in other words, that punishment is one means of preventing violence. However, the overwhelming weight of empirical evidence suggests that exactly the opposite is true—namely, that punishment, far from inhibiting or preventing violence, is the most potent stimulus or cause of violence that we have yet discovered. Several different lines of evidence, from several different populations and stages of the life cycle, converge in supporting that conclusion. For example, child-rearing is such an inherently and inescapably complicated subject that there are relatively few findings from the past several decades of research on it that are so clear, so unmistakable, and so consistently replicated that they are virtually universally agreed on. But among those few is this: the more severely punished children are, the more violent they become, both as children and as adults. This is especially true of violent punishments. For example, children who are subjected to corporal discipline are significantly more likely to subject other people to physical punishments (i.e., inflict violence on them), both while they are still children and after they have reached adulthood. That is hardly surprising, of course, for corporal discipline is simply another name for physical violence; it would be called assault and battery if committed against an adult.

In fact, even with respect to nonviolent behavior, such as bed-wetting or excessive dependency or passivity ("laziness"), punishment has a counterproductive effect; that is, the more severely children are punished for a given behavior, the more strongly they persist in repeating it! To put it the other way around: if we want to produce as violent a generation of children and adults as possible, the most effective thing we can do is to punish our children and adults as severely as possible.

A further piece of evidence that punishment only stimulates violence rather than inhibiting, preventing, or deterring it, can be found from the research on violent child abuse—most of which is committed in the name of discipline, by the way. In other words, almost all the parents who commit violent child abuse on their children perceive what they are doing as exactly what I am saying it is—punishment. The fact is that child abuse is a form of punishment; and punishment (as opposed to restraint) *is* a form of child abuse.

While the research just referred to can be found in the literature on child development and child abuse, there is no reason to think that the psychology of adults differs in this respect from that of children, and every reason to think that it is the same. In fact, I have been able to confirm those findings on children from my own clinical experience of over twenty-five years with violent adult criminals and the violent mentally ill. The degree of violent child abuse to which this population had been subjected was so extreme that the only way to summarize it is to say that the most violent people in our society—those who murder others—are disproportionately the survivors of attempted murder themselves, or of the completed murders of their closest relatives, siblings, or parents. Thus, if punishment would prevent violence, these men would never have become violent in the first place, for they were already punished, even before they became violent, as severely as it is possible to punish a person without actually killing him. Many were beaten nearly to death as children, so when they became adults, they did beat someone else to death.

Further evidence that punishment only stimulates further violence rather than inhibiting or preventing it can be found from my repeated clinical observation that the more severely a prison inmate was punished, the more violent he became. There are undoubtedly several reasons for this. One is that these men regard punishments as both assaults on and tests of their manhood, that is, their adequacy as men. Thus, in order to prove that they are real men, they will go to limitless lengths (to the point of provoking others to beat them into unconsciousness or even death) to prove that they are too strong to be beaten or overcome by any punishment, too courageous to be cowed or deterred by either threatened or actual punishments, and too tough to give in to any degree of pain, no matter how severe.

Another reason punishment provokes violence rather than inhibiting it is that there are two conditions that cause violent behavior, and punishment causes both of those conditions. The first is the experience of shame and humiliation. Nothing stimulates violence as powerfully as the experience of being shamed and humiliated (i.e., disrespected, slighted, insulted, humbled, and mistreated, as if one were a worthless and inferior child rather than a strong and superior man who deserves respect; and treated as though one were weak and cowardly enough to let one's behavior be controlled by fear or pain, i.e., punishment). As the *Oxford English Dictionary* reminds us, it has long been observed that "To punish is properly an act of a superior to an inferior." So to be punished is to be treated as inferior, or in other words, subjected to shame and humiliation, which are precisely the conditions that stimulate violence.

The second condition that leads to violence is the absence of guilt feelings. All of us experience the feeling of being shamed or shameful at one time or another—slighted, insulted, inferior, ridiculed, foolish, disrespected—and that feeling stimulates angry and even violent impulses or fantasies; indeed, there is a consensus in experimental research on the elicitation of anger and of violent impulses and behavior that insulting people is the single most powerful and the most universally effective means of stimulating anger and violence. And yet, even though all of us are slighted or insulted at one time or another, most of us never commit a serious act of violence. What stops most of us, but not some people (such as those who wind up in prison for violent crimes)? Just as the feeling of shame triggers the impulse to hurt someone (that is, to wipe out one's own shame by humiliating someone else), so the impulse to hurt someone triggers the feeling of guilt—in those who have developed and retained the capacity for feeling guilty over such impulses. In fact, the feeling of guilt is one of the most powerful inhibitors of violence toward others, and it is precisely this capacity that is missing in the most violent people. Why is it missing? The simplest answer is that they have been punished severely, frequently, and continuously, beginning in childhood and continuing throughout adulthood. Nothing diminishes guilt feelings as powerfully as punishment does. The church knows that: that is why the practice of penance—a word that has the same root as penitentiary and punishment—has been employed for millennia as a means of diminishing the feeling of sinfulness by magically "undoing" one's guilt. Once you have been punished, according to this psychological logic, you are no longer guilty. So the more severely punished people are, the less guilty they feel, and the more innocent they feel, no matter how "guilty" they may actually be (in legal or moral terms) of whatever acts of violence the penal system punishes them for. Thus punishment creates both of the conditions that cause or stimulate violence: punishment—the infliction of pain—intensifies feelings of shame and diminishes feelings of guilt.

Fortunately, we not only know what stimulates violence (punishment, humiliation), we also know what prevents violence, both in society in general and in the criminal justice and prison systems in particular. Unfortunately, we Americans have been dismantling the conditions that do prevent violence as rapidly as we could over the past twenty years, with the entirely predictable result that the levels of violent crimes, such as murder, have repeatedly reached the highest recorded levels in our history ever since that time. For example, since 1980 our murder rates have been eight to ten times as high as they were at the turn of the century, and eight to ten times as high as they currently are in any other democracy and any other developed economy on earth.

What are the conditions that prevent violence? Among general social conditions, there are several, but space permits mentioning only the most powerful one: a relatively classless society, with an equitable social and economic system in which there are minimal discrepancies in wealth, income, and standard of living between the poorest and the wealthiest fractions of the population (people are vulnerable to feelings of shame and inferiority if they are poor, or economically inferior, while other people are rich, or economically superior). Around the world, the nations with the most equitable economic systems, such as Sweden and Japan, are significantly more likely to have the lowest murder rates (because, among other things, the poor are not that much poorer, and are therefore relatively protected from the most intense feelings of shame and inferiority). And those with the greatest economic discrepancies between the rich and the poor (of which the United States is the world leader among developed economies) have the higest murder rates (a statistic in which the United States is also the world leader). Even within the United States, the most equitable or "classless" states have the lowest murder rates, and those with the most inequitable degrees of class stratification have the highest. Yet the last Congress just dismantled one of the few programs we had that tended to equalize income in this country—the earned income tax credit.

Among the conditions in the prison system that prevent violent behavior (both during imprisonment and after release into the community), the most powerful is education. In Massachusetts, for example, when I headed the prison mental health service, we did a study to see what programs within the prison had been most effective in preventing recidivism, or reoffending, among prison inmates after they had been released from prison and returned to the community. While several programs had worked, the most successful of all and the only one that had been 100 percent effective in preventing recidivism was the program that allowed inmates to receive a college degree while in prison. Several hundred prisoners in Massachusetts had completed at least a bachelor's degree while in prison over a twenty-five-year period, and not one of them had been returned to prison for a new crime. (I later discovered that the state of Indiana and Folsom Prison in California have also found that college degrees provided 100 percent immunity against recidivism among their "alumni.") Immediately after I announced this finding in a public lecture at Harvard and it made its way into the newspapers, our new governor, William Weld, who had not previously been aware that prison inmates could take college courses, gave a press conference on television in which he declared that Massachusetts should rescind that "privilege," or else the poor would start committing crimes in order to be sent to prison so they could get a free college education! And lest one think that that was merely the rather bizarre response of one particularly cynical demagogue, it is worth noting that the U.S. Congress responded the same way. The last Congress declared that inmates throughout the federal prison system would no longer be eligible to receive Pell grants, the funding system that paid the relatively trivial sums of money needed to finance college tuition and textbooks for those too poor to pay for them. And all of that is done in the name of fighting crime and violence!

Truly, it would take a George Orwell to do justice to the reversal of the meanings of ordinary English words in many political debates on violent crime in this country, and to teach us to translate the code language that many (but fortunately not all) politicians use to conceal their thoughts and intentions. In 1984, "war" meant "peace" and "slavery" meant "freedom." In 1996, the "wars" on crime and drugs and the promises to be "tough on crime" and support "family values" are actually means of stimulating violence, subsidizing crime, exacerbating the AIDS epidemic, and destroying American families (by separating millions of fathers from their wives and children, often with life sentences, for the completely nonviolent "crimes" of growing or selling drugs like marijuana and heroin, whose only scientifically demonstrated psychopharmacological effect on violent behavior is to inhibit and prevent violence!).

Perhaps when they reflect on these paradoxes in our society, some of those who contemplate the powerful photographs in this book will wonder why the individuals in prison are those who are pictured here, rather than the politicians who designed the prison system and encourage its expansion. But perhaps the most useful lesson to be derived from these depictions of prisons would be this: that while many prisoners can be reformed, prisons cannot; the prison system itself cannot. Prisons today exist for punishment, and for no other purpose, whatever other uses they may have been intended for in the past. (Prisons, of course, also serve to enrich those who are entrepreneurs in the "correctional-industrial complex" that is currently taking up the slack created by the end of the cold war, and to subsidize whole towns and occupational groups that would otherwise face economic hardship. I am speaking only of the purpose prisons today serve for those who are incarcerated in them.)

It is too late now to even begin to attempt to "reform" prisons. The only thing that can be done with them is to tear them all down, for their architecture alone renders them unfit for human beings. Or even animals: no humane society permits animals in zoos to be housed in conditions as intolerable as those in which we cage humans. The reason for the difference, of course, is clear: zoos are not intended for punishment; prisons are. That is why it would benefit every man, woman, and child in this country, and would hurt no one, to demolish the prisons and replace them with much smaller locked secure residential schools and colleges in which the residents could acquire as much education as their intelligence and curiosity would permit. They would of course be most effective in their only rational purpose, which would be to prevent crime and violence, if they were designed to be as humane and homelike as possible, and as near the prisoners' own homes as possible, so that their families could visit as freely as possible (including with frequent conjugal visits), and so they could visit their families as freely as possible (for conjugal and home visits have repeatedly been shown, in this country and around the world, to be associated with lowered rates of violence, both during incarceration and after release into the community—which is probably why both have been effectively abolished in this country!).

Since there is no reason to isolate anyone from the community against his will unless he poses a danger of physically harming others, these residential schools would need to be limited to those who have been, or have threatened or attempted to be, violent. (Very few if any nonviolent "criminals" need to be removed from the community at all. Nor should those who have committed only nonviolent crimes ever have to be housed with those who have been seriously violent; and there are many reasons why they should not be.)

Thus one of the most constructive responses I can think of to the photographs in this book would be the designing of an "anti-prison"—not prison reform, but prison replacement; not prison construction, but prison deconstruction. If we replaced prisons with a boarding-school "home away from home" for people many of whom were literally homeless in the so-called community, and provide them with the tools they need in order to acquire knowledge and skill, self-esteem and self-respect, and the esteem and respect of others, these new facilities could actually reduce the rates of crime and violence in our society, instead of feeding them as our current prisons do.

Of course, before we could do that we would need to overcome our own irrational need to inflict revenge (i.e., punishment) on those who are weaker than we. Nothing corrodes the soul of the vengeful person as thoroughly as his own vengeful impulses. Thus the main reason we need to abolish the kind of institution depicted in this book of photographs is not only, or even primarily, for the sake of those who get imprisoned in them, but in order to heal our own souls—and indeed, our whole society, which is sick with an epidemic of violence, both legal and illegal.

Behind the Razor Wire

The degree of civilization in a society can be judged by entering its prisons.

—Fyodor Dostoyevsky

Charles Street Jail, Boston, Massachusetts, 1993

Prison is a dead man's zone.

Look into the eyes of men here,

There is something more than cautiousness,

A sense of complete cold barren knowledge,

Of being abused too long and too far,

Coerced into indignities that pile up on them,

Into conditions that make them reckless and savage,

Watching the Directors of Prisons on TV

Fiddle with lies, sliding past the truth

That really exists here, the impending violence . . .

Turning around and around us daily

Like a gigantic snake slowly choking us,

Sinking its fangs as the poison seeps deep

Day to day in this Arena of Death,

Where Hope seeps through the cracks of our dark skulls,

And lights go on to start another day,

As if nothing at all had happened last night.

—*Jimmy Santiago Baca, "Overcrowding"*

Prisoner at North Central Correctional Institution,   43
Gardner, Massachusetts, 1992

44

One in three black men aged 20-29 are reportedly under some form of criminal justice supervision.

—The Sentencing Project, 1995

Prisoner at Deer Island jail, Winthrop, Massachusetts,   45
1991

Our rate of criminal violence is a consequence of choices that we have made in this country as to how to share, or not share, our collective wealth. And we are paying the price for those choices. We can continue to pay that price if we want to, but what we cannot do is to continue the high degree of class stratification and expect to have less criminal violence, because the one directly causes the other.

—James Gilligan, M.D., former director of mental health for the

Massachusetts prison system, 1996

Prisoners at North Central Correctional Institution, Gardner, Massachusetts, 1993

48

The big compound gates close the world off,
Lock with a thunderous thud and clunk,
While bits of dust scatter into your lungs,
Breathing in the first stark glance
Of prison cellblocks behind the great wall,
Breathing in the emptiness, the darkness
As you walk with an easy step on the cold sidewalk.

Then another door locks behind you.
This door is your cell door. A set of bars,
Paint scraped, still as cobras in gray skins,
Wrapping around your heart little by little:
The ones you love cannot be touched,
Christmas, Easter, Valentine's Day, Mother's Day,
All seen from these bars, celebrated
With a deep laboring yearning within,
While the cobras slowly wind and choke
Your mind, your heart, your spirit,
You hear nothing but the steel jaws close,
Slowly swallowing you.

—Jimmy Santiago Baca, "Steel Doors of Prison"

Prisoner at Hampden County House of Correction (York   49
Street jail), Springfield, Massachusetts, 1992

Being touched & scarred
in my childhood home
behind the walls of untold lust.
No real emotion.
Only fear & darkness.
Screams
before school & night
between bed & morning.
　　　—Janice Barnes, "Earliest Memory"

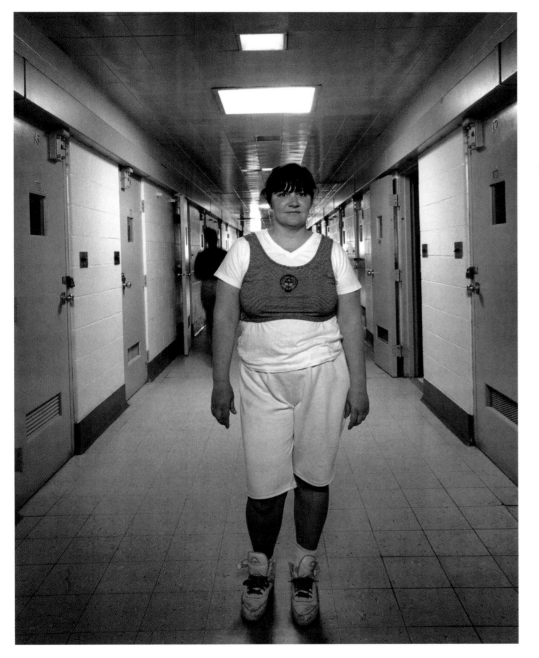

Prisoner at MCI–Framingham, Massachusetts, 1992　　　51

The number of female inmates increased at a faster rate during 1993 than the number of male inmates.   *—U.S. Department of Justice, 1995*

Prisoners in modular unit at MCI–Framingham, Massachusetts, 1992

The night a young woman hung herself in the max-unit, many others cried. For days and days and weeks, everyone was upset. There was a Catholic mass said for her. The administration allowed us to gather under the windows where it happened. She was a frightened and confused person who needed help. Instead, she was locked in a room, the door shut. Put in seclusion. She was a new mother. Yet she chose to leave her small daughter behind. She hadn't been found guilty by the courts yet—she was still awaiting sentencing—or perhaps she would have been set free?

Perhaps she only meant to alarm everyone—and not actually die. The officers couldn't, or didn't, save her. They tried to run things as if nothing had happened that night. Something had —a little piece of everyone died with the realization of how fragile reality is, how cruel it is to lock up human beings as if they were animals.

—Anonymous, from The World Split Open

Isolation unit no longer in use at MCI–Framingham, 55
Massachusetts, 1992

Every prison . . .
Is built with bricks of shame,
And bound with bars lest Christ should see
How men their brothers maim.

With bars that blur the gravous moon,
And blind the goodly sun;
And they do well to hide their hell,
For in it things are done
That Son of God nor Son of Man
Ever should look upon!

The violent deeds like poison weeds
Bloom well in prison-air.
It is only what is good in man
That wastes and withers there.

    —Oscar Wilde, The Ballad of Reading Gaol

Cells no longer in use at MCI–Framingham, Massachusetts, 1992

Now I am faced with a new set of problems which stem from my present incarceration. It is hard to live in a half existence and that is where I am at. I no longer look at a chain link fence with deadly razor wire running around the top. I no longer am forced to go to my room and be counted, I no longer must be locked away deeper in a room at an appointed time, but I still feel, taste, and live the horror of this nightmare. Yes this lonely hideous nightmare has a name, it has a face, it has an invisible fence and this nightmare is called prison living. The only problem is it is not a bad dream but a prominent reality I must live.

—Lisa Odell, "Uphill Battle"

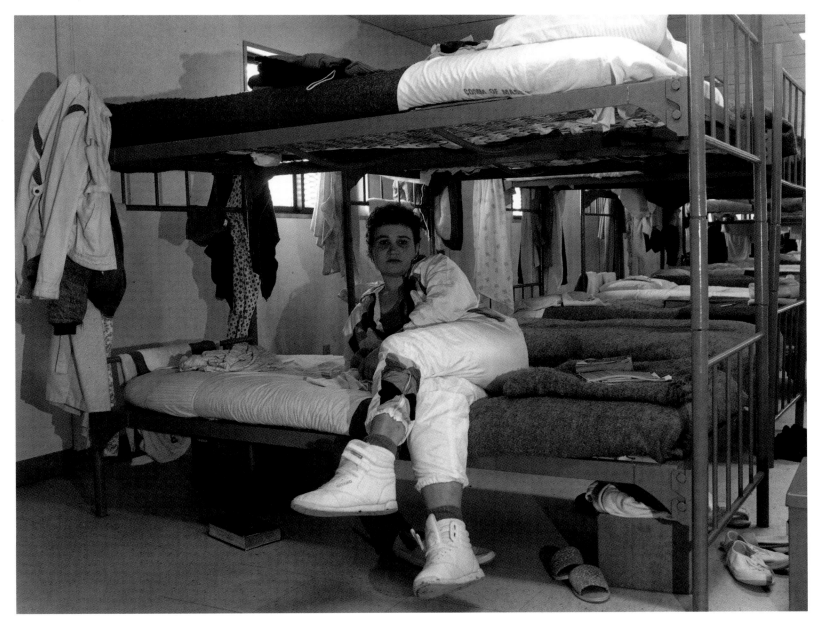

Prisoner at MCI–Framingham, Massachusetts, 1992

Lonely, oh yes I could probably write as well as any expert on the subject and quite extensively. Loneliness is needing someone to share your feelings with but there is no one there.

Loneliness is the feeling of your tears burning down your face but there is no comfort in sight so you are left to console your self. . . .

Loneliness is being separated from your children and they in turn separated from one another. I could go on and on and on but at this time I feel it is best I stop. Pain is beginning to seep through and my eyes are filled. So I will leave my thoughts here on this page, turn in, and attempt to get some sleep alone once again.

—Lisa Odell, "Uphill Battle"

Prisoner at MCI–Framingham, Massachusetts, 1992

As poor African-Americans began migrating to the northern cities at the end of the nineteenth century and then in bigger and bigger waves during World War I and the 1920s, it might have seemed likely that they would adopt the new ways of the metropolis. But blacks were largely shut out of jobs in the industrial economy, and therefore did not share in its new values. They were isolated by discrimination, high unemployment, bad schools, and unsafe neighborhoods. . . . In these desperate conditions, Southern-born honor found a new spawning ground. Honor became even more dangerous when combined with poverty, racism, and big-city slums.

—*Fox Butterfield*, All God's Children

Prisoner at North Central Correctional Institution,   63
Gardner, Massachusetts, 1993

He chose the bright lights winking right in front of his face, just beyond his fingertips. For him and most of his buddies, "normal" was poverty, drugs, street crime, Vietnam, or prison.

—*John Edgar Wideman,* Brothers and Keepers

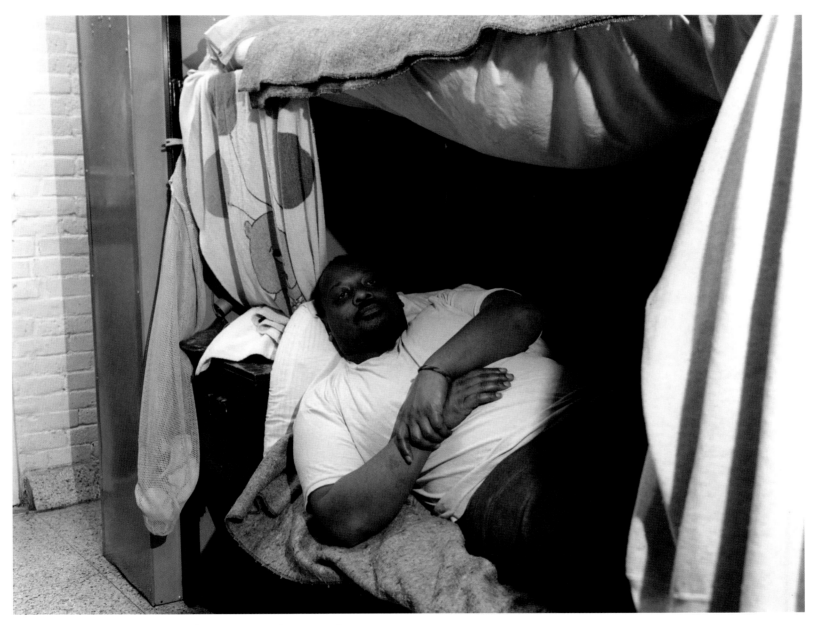

Prisoner at North Central Correctional Institution, Gardner, Massachusetts, 1993

The percentage of Hispanics in the state and federal prison system has doubled from 1980 to 1993, rising from 7.7 percent to 14.3 percent.

—The Sentencing Project, 1995

Hampden County House of Correction, Ludlow, Massachusetts, 1994

The idea of prisoners as victims is one which doesn't lend itself to much support these days. The mentality out there in the free world is one of retribution and extended incarceration. Be that as it may, the fact remains that most prisoners are just that: victims. No one is born a criminal. I don't believe in the "bad seed" scenario. No, criminals are created, not born. They are fostered in the furnace of own, what they earn, as opposed to who they are. They are created in infernos of child abuse, poverty, status degradation, sexual abuse. The list is a long one, and one full of misery and pain.

—Arthur DeTullio, prisoner at MCI–Norfolk, 1992

Prisoners at Hampden County House of Correction, Ludlow, Massachusetts, 1994

Prisons in this country are used mainly for those who commit a select group of crimes, primarily burglary, robbery, larceny, and assault. Excluded are the criminals of the capitalist class, who cause more of an economic and social loss to the country and the society but who are not often given prison sentences. This means that prisons are institutions of control for the working class, especially the surplus population of the working class.

—Richard Quinney, "The Political Economy of Criminal Justice"

Family waiting outside the "Pedestrian Trap" at Deer Island jail, Winthrop, Massachusetts, 1991

For local jails in 1994, the incarceration rate among blacks was almost 6 times that among whites.

—U.S. Department of Justice, 1995

Prisoner at Hampden County House of Correction (York   73
Street jail), Springfield, Massachusetts, 1992

My mother was a drug addict. She used to get high and party. She was on heroin. I remember going with her to the methadone clinic in Holyoke. She sold our home to support her drug habit. I lived in a tent with my stepfather the summer that she was hospitalized. I was loyal to her till the end. She died in a fire when I was twenty-one.

—Crispin Mathieu, prisoner at Hampshire County House of Correction, 1996

Crispin Mathieu at Hampshire County House of Correction, Northampton, Massachusetts, 1996

I got caught selling drugs—possession with intent. In '88 I went to MCI-Framingham for the same charges and I did six months out of a year. I grew up without a father. My mother brought six children up. I grew up in a family with alcohol. That's all I learned to do, use and abuse. I grew up in a poor neighborhood and that's all I saw. I started drinking when I was nine years old. I went on to heroin and cocaine. I had five kids by the age of twenty. I hope that when I get out, I'll do something different with my life and with my children. It's painful being away from my kids. I have a daughter that writes to me. She's thirteen years old and writes, "I miss you. I want to be with you." She says the rest of her family doesn't understand her. They're all into drugs. Every time I hear from her she's getting kicked out of here and sent over there. It's hard for me because I don't want to see her in a foster home. I have two kids that are in foster care.

—Emily Olivo, prisoner at Hampden County House of Correction, 1994

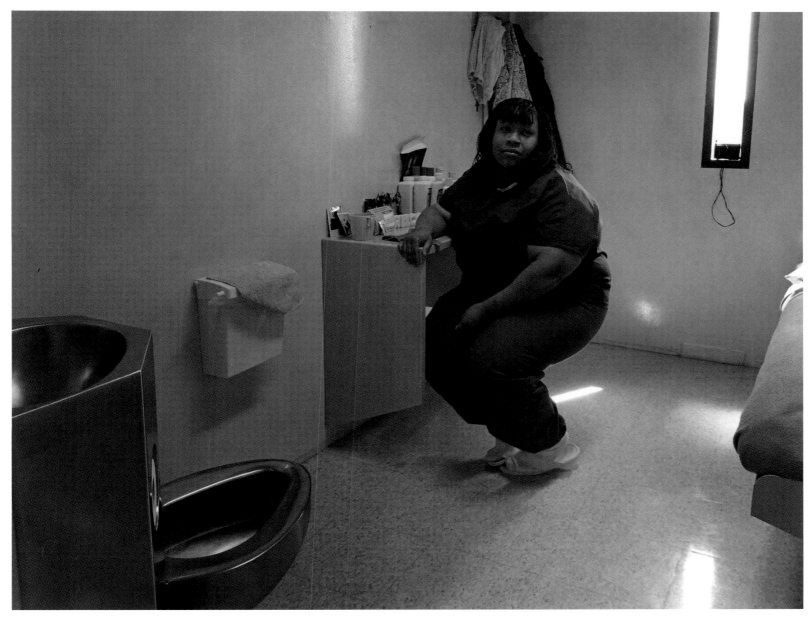

Emily Olivo at Hampden County House of Correction, Ludlow, Massachusetts, 1994

I come from a poor family. My father was a foundry worker. My mother was a housewife. I grew up in a violent home where both parents were alcoholics and drug addicts. My dad worked hard. He always worked. He never did care too much for himself but he provided for the family. When he got to drinking he always wanted to fight. He liked to punch, kick, sometimes he used boards or broom sticks, belt buckles. I always felt insecure around him. There were times when we were taken away from our family by the state. My mother tried to kill herself many times. She felt unworthy of life. She thinks she failed with us. My brothers and I all turned out with some kind of drug or alcohol addiction. Me and one other brother did some extensive time. We all dropped out of school. I went to reform school when I was fourteen years old. I've been in and out of prison several times. I felt the need to be somebody. I felt unworthy when I was around my family because I was always being put down—so I didn't feel like I was anybody. I had to show someone that I am somebody—to draw some kind of attention to myself by my name or picture being in the newspaper. I was looking for something. I never found fulfillment in my life.

—Terry Moran, prisoner at Hampden County House of Correction, 1994

Terry Moran at Hampden County House of Correction, Ludlow, Massachusetts, 1994

In 1993 illness was the leading cause of death in local jails (45%), followed by suicide (36%). Acquired immune deficiency syndrome (AIDS) accounted for about 10% of reported inmate deaths; homicide, 3%; and other causes, 6%.

—U.S. Department of Justice, 1995

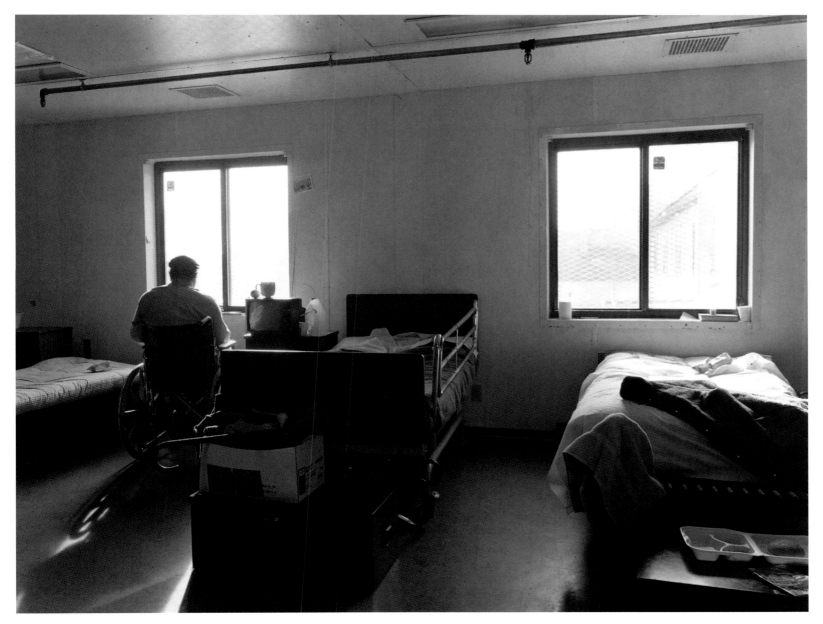

Infirmary at Deer Island jail, Winthrop, Massachusetts, 1991

I've been in and out of prison many times. I got AIDS from using dirty needles.

—Prisoner at MCI–Framingham, 1992 (on left in photo on opposite page)

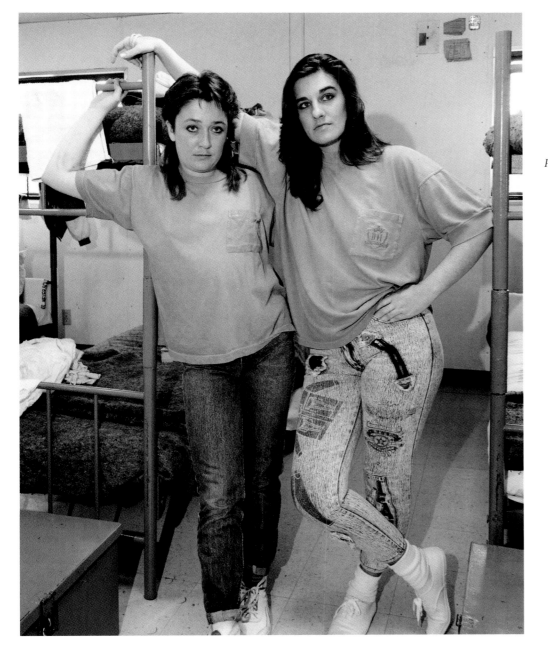

Prisoners at MCI–Framingham, Massachusetts, 1992   83

Forty-four percent of the state prisoners in Massachusetts had served one or more sentences in a county jail. — *Massachusetts Department of Corrections, 1995*

Recidivism rates were highest in the first 2 years after an offender's release from prison. Within 1 year, 32% of those paroled had been rearrested; within 2 years, 47% had been rearrested. — *U.S. Department of Justice, 1987*

"I'll Get Out" at Deer Island jail, Winthrop, 85
Massachusetts, 1991

The Commonwealth has made a staggering financial investment in its criminal justice system during the last decade. In both capital outlays and operating budgets, the system's expenditures are consuming an escalating share of our shrinking state resources. Since 1980, the state has spent more than $1 billion in capital expenditures on corrections. . . . However, these massive capital outlays have done little to relieve prison and jail crowding. . . . Moreover, it is clear that the Commonwealth's troubled times make it virtually impossible to build our way out of this crisis in the 1990s.

—Boston Bar Association and Crime and Justice Foundation, 1991

Prison yard at MCI–Cedar Junction, Walpole, Massachusetts, 1993

In 1992 the operating budget for MCI Cedar Junction was $18,815,058 and the cost of housing an inmate at MCI Cedar Junction was $22,812.52 per year.

—MCI–Cedar Junction Media Booklet

Prisoner at MCI–Cedar Junction, Walpole, Massachusetts, 1993

I'm of the belief that prison should be like a tour through the circles of hell. . . . Further, as a check on the problem of recidivism, prison should, as I said during my campaign, "reintroduce inmates to the joys of busting rocks."

—*Governor William Weld, speech at the*

U.S. Attorney General's Summit on Corrections, April 27, 1992

Ten Block at MCI–Cedar Junction, Walpole, Massachusetts, 1993

Is it surprising that prisons resemble factories, schools, barracks, hospitals, which all resemble prisons?

—*Michel Foucault,* Discipline and Punish

Departmental Disciplinary Unit Control Center at MCI–Cedar Junction, Walpole, Massachusetts, 1993

In the 1980s the need for a new segregation unit was established and on January 23, 1992, the DDU was opened for occupancy with a design capacity for 120 inmates. It is the sincere hope of the Department that inmates will conform their conduct to a minimum level of good behavior and leave the DDU at less than full occupancy, however, that choice will be up to the inmate.

—MCI–Cedar Junction Media Booklet

Departmental Disciplinary Unit sensory deprivation   95
cells, where prisoners are locked up twenty-three hours a
day, MCI–Cedar Junction, Walpole, Massachusetts, 1993

In essence, the DDU is reserved for those inmates who are deemed to have committed a particularly serious offense or set of offenses. A sentence to the DDU is designed to punish and thereby deter serious misbehavior by inmates in the Department's general population.

—MCI–Cedar Junction Media Booklet

Recreation is confined to walks in the "kennel," one hour a day, five days a week. The men are frequently handcuffed during their exercise period. Departmental Disciplinary Unit, MCI–Cedar Junction, Walpole, Massachusetts, 1993

Downward social mobility, unemployment, and homelessness are among the most potent stimuli of shame, and are a key to the politics of violence.

—*James Gilligan, M.D.,* Violence: Our Deadly Epidemic and Its Causes

The deadliest form of violence is poverty.

—*Gandhi*

Shotgun tower at MCI–Cedar Junction, Walpole, Massachusetts, 1993

The moral and ethical principles that bind society don't count inside prison. You, the custodians, formulate whatever rules, whatever system you require to keep the prisoners in captivity. You must stand between them and us. You are not a connection between the free world and the prison world but a chasm, a wall, a two-sided, unbreakable mirror. When we look at you we see ourselves. We see order and justice. Your uniforms, your rules reflect humane discipline. We see our faces, a necessarily severe aspect of our nature in the stern mask above your martial attire. When prisoners gaze into the reverse side of the mirror they should see the deformed aberrations they've become. Keepers are set in place to reflect and sustain this duality. In between the bright mirrors stretches an abyss.

—*John Edgar Wideman*, Brothers and Keepers

Prison guard at MCI–Cedar Junction, Walpole, Massachusetts, 1993

An estimated 4.8 million adults were under some form of correctional supervision in 1992. Local jails held an estimated 442,000 adults, or about 1 in every 428 adult U.S. residents, on June 30, 1992. The total number of adults in jail increased 142% in the 12 years from 1980 to 1992, including an increase of 4.2% from 1991 to 1992.

On June 30, 1995, state prisons held 1,004,608 inmates and federal prisons held 99,466. About 95% of all prisoners were men; 48% were white, and 50%, black.

Between 1980 and 1994 the total number of people held in federal and state prisons and local jails almost tripled—increasing from 501,886 to 1,483,410. As of December 31, 1994, the total incarceration rate reached 565 inmates per 100,000 U.S. residents.

—U.S. Department of Justice, 1995

Prison guard at MCI–Cedar Junction, Walpole, Massachusetts, 1993

Between 1983 and 1993 the number of jail inmates increased 106%; the total jail staff increased 156%; and the number of correctional officers grew 165%.

—U.S. Department of Justice, 1995

Prison guard at Hampden County House of Correction, Ludlow, Massachusetts, 1994

During the past 12 months the state prison population grew by 9.1 percent and the federal prison population by 6.1 percent, which is the equivalent of 1,725 new prison beds every week.

—U.S. Department of Justice, 1995

The finding is clear: the prison population increases as the rate of unemployment increases. . . . A way of controlling this unemployed surplus population is simply and directly by confinement in prisons.

—Richard Quinney, "The Political Economy of Criminal Justice"

Prison guards at MCI–Shirley, Massachusetts, 1993

As of 1990, the U.S. spent approximately $74 billion each year to operate the nation's criminal justice system.

      —John Irwin and James Austin, It's About Time: America's Imprisonment Binge

Prison yard at Hampden County House of Correction, Ludlow, Massachusetts, 1994

During the King Philip's War of 1675-76, the Massachusetts Bay Colony began using Deer Island to house society's unwanted. . . . After the war, Native Americans were imprisoned on the Island and sold into slavery in the West Indies. In the mid-19th century, Deer Island became an asylum for the city's social and economic outcasts. . . . The primary adult inmates of the House of Industry were sentenced by the courts to serve time at Deer Island for misdemeanors and for crimes committed in the city of Boston, including drunkenness and idleness.

—*Massachusetts Water Resources Authority, "History of Deer Island"*

Three tiers of cells in maximum-security section of Deer Island jail, Winthrop, Massachusetts, 1991   111

They turn the water off, so I live without water,

they build walls higher, so I live without treetops,

they paint the windows black, so I live without sunshine,

they lock my cage, so I live without going anywhere,

they take each last tear I have, I live without tears,

they take my heart and rip it open, I live without heart,

they take my life and crush it, so I live without a future,

they say I am beastly and fiendish, so I have no friends,

they stop up each hope, so I have no passage out of hell,

they give me pain, so I live with pain,

they give me hate, so I live with my hate,

they have changed me, and I am not the same man,

they give me no shower, so I live with my smell,

they separate me from my brothers, so I live without brothers.

—Jimmy Santiago Baca, "Who Understands Me but Me"

Prisoner at Hampden County House of Correction (York Street jail), Springfield, Massachusetts, 1992 113

They all express being different, dropping out of school in the fourth or sixth grade. That's the educational level that I teach. So they didn't stay in school for very long. With no skills they went into the drug culture. Most of our inmates have been traumatized in childhood by neglect, physical abuse, mental abuse.

—Ruth Connors, substance abuse educator and program planner for the Hampden County Sheriff's Department, 1994

Library and church at Hampden County House of Correction (York Street jail), Springfield, Massachusetts, 1992

Prisoner sewing uniform at Hampden County House of Correction, Ludlow, Massachusetts, 1994

Ense petit placidam sub libertate queitem:
[By the sword we seek peace, but peace only
under liberty.]

117

—Massachusetts State Flag

Prisoner silk-screening the Massachusetts state flag
at MCI–Cedar Junction, Walpole, Massachusetts, 1993

118

Prisoner making license plates at MCI–Cedar Junction, Walpole, Massachusetts, 1993

Prisoner making license plates at MCI–Cedar Junction,   119
Walpole, Massachusetts, 1993

Prisoner ironing uniforms at MCI–Cedar Junction, Walpole, Massachusetts, 1993

Prisoner sewing the American flag at MCI–Framingham, Massachusetts, 1993

It is utter folly to imagine that prison can correct something, especially something as profound as the ills of a whole society. These ills, for the most part, are heaped part and parcel upon the underclass, who invariably fill up the prison cages. Prison exists primarily for the poor. It's insane to imagine that only the poor commit crimes, yet they make up the vast percentage of America's prison population. I have met damn few millionaires walking the yard!

—Arthur DeTullio, prisoner at MCI–Norfolk, 1992

Men at Work, Hampden County House of Correction   123
(York Street jail), Springfield, Massachusetts, 1992

Local jails throughout the United States spent over $9.6 billion during the year ending June 30, 1993. This estimated total (not adjusted for inflation) was more than double the $2.7 billion spent in 1983. The Northeast had the highest average operating expenditure per inmate ($22,678).

—U.S. Department of Justice, 1995

$75 million Hampden County House of Correction, Ludlow, Massachusetts, 1994

Prison is a repository of human misery; a warehouse of broken, damaged, twisted human be-ings operating out of impulses most don't even understand.

—Arthur DeTullio, prisoner at MCI–Norfolk, 1992

Deer Island jail, Winthrop, Massachusetts, 1991   127

While there is a lower class, I am in it; while there is a criminal element, I am of it; while there is a soul in prison, I am not free.

—*Eugene Debs*

Prisoner at MCI–Framingham, Massachusetts, 1993

Contributors

Angela Y. Davis has been writing and organizing around prison issues for the last three decades. In the early 1970s she was one of the most celebrated political prisoners in the United States. Since her acquittal in 1972 on false charges of murder, kidnapping, and conspiracy, she has worked continuously as an educator, activist, and author. She is a professor in the History of Consciousness Department at the University of California at Santa Cruz.

James Gilligan, M.D., is an author of *Violence: Our Deadly Epidemic and Its Causes* and the former director of mental health for the Massachusetts prison system. He has worked clinically with violent men for over twenty-five years, and directed the Center for the Study of Violence and the Institute of Law and Psychiatry at Harvard Medical School, where he has been on the faculty since 1966.

Michael Jacobson-Hardy's photographs have been exhibited widely and are included in many public and private collections, including the Smithsonian Institution, the Henry Ford Museum, the Yale University Art Gallery, and the Rose Art Museum at Brandeis University. He is author of *The Changing Landscape of Labor: American Workers and Workplaces* (University of Massachusetts Press, 1996).

Marc Mauer is the assistant director of The Sentencing Project, a national nonprofit organization engaging in research and advocacy on criminal justice policy.

John Edgar Wideman is a professor of English at the University of Massachusetts and the recipient of the prestigious PEN/Faulkner Award. He is the author of *Brothers and Keepers* and *Fatheralong*.

Copyright Information

Jimmy Santiago Baca, "Overcrowding," "Steel Doors of Prison," and "Who Understands Me but Me," from *What's Happening* (Curbstone Press). © 1982. Reprinted by permission.

Janice Barnes, "Earliest Memory," from *Inspired in Prison: Writing and Art* (Connecticut Prison Association). © 1994–95.

Boston Bar Association and Crime and Justice Foundation, "The Crisis in Corrections and Sentencing in Massachusetts." © 1991.

Fox Butterfield, *All God's Children: The Bosket Family and the American Tradition of Violence* (Knopf). © 1995.

Michel Foucault, *Discipline and Punish* (Vintage). © 1995.

James Gilligan, M.D., *Violence: Our Deadly Epidemic and Its Causes* (Grosset/Putnam). © 1996. Interview in *Boston Globe*, April 17, 1996.

John Irwin and James Austin, *It's About Time: America's Imprisonment Binge* (Wadsworth). © 1994.

Massachusetts Department of Corrections, The Background Characteristics and Recidivism Rates for Releases from Massachusetts Correctional Institutions, 1991. © 1995.

Massachusetts Water Resources Authority, "History of Deer Island." © 1991.

MCI–Cedar Junction Media Booklet, Walpole, MA. © 1992.

Lisa Odell, "Uphill Battle," from *The World Split Open: Writing and Theatre by Women in Prison* (Cultural Images Group). © 1992. Reprinted by permission.

Richard Quinney, "The Political Economy of Criminal Justice," from *Class, State, and Crime* (Longman). © 1977.

The Sentencing Project, "Young Black Americans and the Criminal Justice System: Five Years Later." © 1995.

John Edgar Wideman, *Brothers and Keepers* (Vintage). © 1995. "Doing Time, Marking Race" © 1995, first printed in the *Nation* and reprinted with permission of the Wylie Agency, Inc.

The World Split Open: Writing and Theatre by Women in Prison (Cultural Images Group). © 1992. Reprinted by permission.